DIEPPE 1942

DIEPPE 1942

OPERATION JUBILEE – A LEARNING CURVE

STEPHEN WYNN

Pen & Sword
MILITARY

AN IMPRINT OF PEN & SWORD BOOKS LTD.
YORKSHIRE – PHILADELPHIA

First published in Great Britain in 2023 by
Pen & Sword Military
An imprint of
Pen & Sword Books Ltd
Yorkshire - Philadelphia

Copyright © Stephen Wynn, 2023

ISBN 978 1 52671 481 7

The right of Stephen Wynn to be identified as the Author of this work has been asserted by him in accordance with the Copyright, Designs and Patents Act 1988.

A CIP catalogue record for this book is available from the British Library.

All rights reserved. No part of this book may be reproduced or transmitted in any form or by any means, electronic or mechanical, including photocopying, recording or by any information storage and retrieval system, without permission from the Publisher in writing.

Typeset in INDIA by IMPEC eSolutions
Printed and bound in England by CPI Group (UK) Ltd., Croydon, CR0 4YY

Pen & Sword Books Ltd. incorporates the Imprints of Pen & Sword Archaeology, Atlas, Aviation, Battleground, Discovery, Family History, History, Maritime, Military, Naval, Politics, Railways, Select, Transport, True Crime, Fiction, Frontline Books, Leo Cooper, Praetorian Press, Seaforth Publishing, Wharncliffe, White Owl and After the Battle.

For a complete list of Pen & Sword titles please contact

PEN & SWORD BOOKS LIMITED
47 Church Street, Barnsley, South Yorkshire, S70 2AS, England
E-mail: enquiries@pen-and-sword.co.uk
Website: www.pen-and-sword.co.uk

or

PEN AND SWORD BOOKS
1950 Lawrence Rd, Havertown, PA 19083, USA
E-mail: uspen-and-sword@casematepublishers.com
Website: www.penandswordbooks.com

Contents

Acknowledgements		vii
Chapter One	Dieppe: The Build Up	1
Chapter Two	Operation Rutter	14
Chapter Three	The Raid on Dieppe	25
Chapter Four	RAF Flight Sergeant Jack Nissenthall	45
Chapter Five	1st Battalion, US Army Rangers at Dieppe	62
Chapter Six	French Civilians and the Dieppe Raid	66
Chapter Seven	German Defenders at Dieppe	71
Chapter Eight	The RAF and the Dieppe Raid	80
Chapter Nine	The Essex Scottish Regiment and the Rivait Brothers	85
Chapter Ten	Military Awards of the Dieppe Raid	90
Chapter Eleven	The German Perception of the Raid	105
Chapter Twelve	The Dieppe Raid in the News	110
Chapter Thirteen	The Enigma Pinch	134
Chapter Fourteen	1er Bataillon de Fusiliers Marins Commandos	139
Chapter Fifteen	Canadian Military Report No. 83 – 19 September 1942	144
Chapter Sixteen	Canadian Military Report No. 100 – 16 July 1943	162
Chapter Seventeen	Canadian Military Report No. 142 – 18 July 1945	173
Chapter Eighteen	The Raid Seen Through 'Open Eyes'	192
Chapter Nineteen	Beach Comber the Homing Pigeon	201

Conclusion	205
Appendix A: Forces Deployed at Dieppe	216
Appendix B: Men of No. 3 Commando Killed at Dieppe	224
Appendix C: Men of the South Saskatchewan Regiment Killed at Dieppe	227
Appendix D: Men of the Queen's Own Cameron Highlanders of Canada Killed at Dieppe	231
Appendix E: Men of the Black Watch (Royal Highland Regiment of Canada) Killed at Dieppe	234
Appendix F: Decorations Awarded Following the Dieppe Raid	235
Appendix G: French Civilians Killed in the Dieppe Raid	242
Sources	244
About the Author	245
Index	247

Acknowledgements

Linda Nissen Samuels, daughter of Sergeant Jack Nissenthall, for her help and assistance with her father's story.

Susan Sorby-Gitchell, for her valuable assistance in providing detailed information on the members of the 1st Battalion, United States Rangers, who took part in the raid on Dieppe. Her uncle, Tom A. Sorby, was one of the Rangers involved.

Gregory Salmers, webmaster of the South Saskatchewan Regiment website, hosted by Saskatchewan Military Museum.

Daniel Jaspart, the administrator of the Jubilee Association Memorial in Dieppe, for his permission to use a photograph of the memorial listing French civilians killed during the raid on Dieppe.

Introduction

The first potential question that comes to mind when thinking about the raid on Dieppe, or to refer to it by its official title, Operation Jubilee, is why? What was its purpose? What did it achieve and was the cost paid in human life actually worth it?

This book will ultimately answer that question by looking at who devised the plan, who approved it, and what it achieved when measured against the eventual outcome of the war. It will also consider the regiments and units that took part in the raid, how many were killed, what – if anything – was learned from it, and why it ultimately failed.

As history has recorded, the raid was an Allied defeat: the result of blunders rather than the superiority of a stronger enemy. It was a raid that resulted in approximately 1,200 men being killed and nearly 2,500 more wounded, with a further 2,000 taken as prisoners, destined to spend the rest of the war incarcerated in prisoner of war camps deep in the German heartland.

The raid on Dieppe took place on Wednesday, 19 August 1942. By this time the war was three years old and Britain and her Allies had been having a torrid time of things. The campaign in Norway between April and June 1940 had not ended well, with British forces sustaining nearly 4,500, casualties, and France, Poland and Norwegian forces collectively loosing 1,400 men killed.

Between May and June 1940, the evacuations of some 338,000 British and Commonwealth troops had taken place on the beaches of Dunkirk. The Battle of Britain had raged backwards and forwards for four months between July and October the same year, and Britain was already on to its second prime minister of the war.

The Blitz, involving a number of air raids on towns and cities across the UK by aircraft of the German Luftwaffe, took place between 7 September 1940 and 11 May 1941. These raids resulted in the deaths of an estimated 43,000 civilians, with between 46,000 and 139,000 others seriously injured. It is estimated that somewhere in the region of 2 million homes were either damaged or destroyed, with 1.2 million of these being in London.

From 7 September 1940, the Luftwaffe bombed British towns and cities for fifty-six of the next fifty-seven days. Ports in Hull, Bristol, Cardiff, Portsmouth, Plymouth, Southampton, Belfast and Glasgow were all targeted, along with the industrial areas of Birmingham, Coventry, Manchester and Sheffield.

The last major aerial attack on London took place on the night of 10/11 May 1941, in which 1,436 people were killed. These attacks badly affected the morale of the UK's civilian population.

Meanwhile, February 1942 had seen the loss of an estimated 90,000 British and Commonwealth forces captured by the Japanese at Singapore.

What the effect of another military loss would be on the British public was unclear. Nevertheless, Nazism needed to be defeated once and for all, and there would be no second chances.

CHAPTER ONE

Dieppe: The Build Up

Winston Churchill's memoirs of the Second World War were first published in 1958 and included his thoughts on the raid on Dieppe on 19 August 1942:

> I thought it most important that a large scale operation should take place this summer, and military opinion seemed unanimous that until an operation on that scale was undertaken, no responsible general would take the responsibility of planning the main invasion. In discussion with Admiral Mountbatten, it became clear that time did not permit a new scale operation to be mounted during the summer (after "Rutter" had been cancelled), but that Dieppe could be remounted (with the new code-name "Jubilee") within a month, provided extraordinary steps were taken to ensure secrecy. For this reason, no records were kept but, after the Canadian authorities and the Chiefs of Staff had given their approval, I personally went through the plans with the C.I.G.S. [Chief of the Imperial General Staff], Admiral Mountbatten, and the Naval Commander, Captain J. Hughes-Hallett.

The other men involved in organising the Dieppe Raid were Canadian Army Officer Major General John Hamilton Roberts, and Air Chief Marshal Sir Trafford Leigh-Mallory of the Royal Air Force. Lieutenant General Bernard Montgomery was initially also part of the organising group, but because of his concerns over the potential dangers of carrying out such an operation, he withdrew. The effect this had on his colleagues can only be guessed at.

The lack of any mention in Churchill's memoirs about Dieppe on the opening up of a second front in an effort to try to draw German forces away from the East and their fight with Soviet forces was noticeable by its omission, although there was mention about the planning for a subsequent 'main invasion'.

Certainly, at the time, and from a subsequent historical perspective, it has been accepted that one of the reasons behind the raid taking place was to open up a second front and, in doing so, help to take the pressure away from Soviet forces in the East, both to appease Stalin and to prove that Britain, and America, were committed and supportive allies.

The plan for the Dieppe Raid, remembering of course Churchill's own admission that 'no records were kept', was to attack and capture the harbour and seafront areas, hold them for an unspecified period of time, and land military vehicles (such as tanks) on the beach to gauge the feasibility for the future landings of large numbers of vehicles of all descriptions as part of the main Allied invasion of Europe. In addition, military intelligence was to be gathered, German defences were to be eliminated and the harbour area left unusable for the foreseeable future. The raid's additional aim was an attempt to try to raise morale amongst British civilians after what had been a damaging first three years of the war.

The idea for the raid on Dieppe was realistic and the plan reasonably well thought through, but it was flawed in part from the very beginning because the intelligence used to direct the planning was extremely poor.

It was Winston Churchill himself who was behind the idea of carrying out such raids against nominated locations along the coastline of German-occupied Europe. To undertake these operations, the War Office set up the Combined Operations Headquarters, which came into being on 17 July 1940, with Admiral of the Fleet Roger Keyes put in charge. However, his tenure only lasted fifteen months because as well as having fallen out of favour with Churchill, he was deemed to be somewhat unrealistic in his ideas for what operations should be undertaken. He was replaced by a favourite of Churchill, Lord Louis Mountbatten, on 27 October 1941, and would hold the position until October 1943, when he was succeeded by Major General Sir Robert Laycock.

The main purpose of this new and progressive unit, which was officially a department of the War Office in Whitehall, was to harass German forces along the coastline of occupied Europe by carrying out Commando raids against nominated military targets. To achieve this goal, all three wings of the British military, the Army, Royal Air Force and the Royal Navy, all had to work in unison. Although it would be the Army who carried out the raids, the RAF would provide air support and the Navy would be the ones to deliver the men to, and pick them up from, their target area.

Once a location had been identified as a potential target, the raid itself had to be planned. This part was undertaken by high-ranking officers from within the Combined Operations Headquarters. However, Dieppe was different from any previous Commando raid that had been carried out because for the first time, the intention was to land tanks on a foreign beach.

The men involved in the Dieppe Raid, including those in charge of planning it, were as follows:

Admiral Louis Mountbatten

Mountbatten began his distinguished naval career as midshipman in July 1916 on board the Royal Navy's battlecruiser HMS *Lion*. He came from an illustrious background and had as his grandmother none other than Queen Victoria, who was also one of his godparents, along with Tsar Nicholas II of Russia.

In the latter stages of the First World War, he also served on board the Royal Navy's battleship HMS *Queen Elizabeth*, which was often used as a flagship.

He remained in the Navy during the interwar years, gradually rising through the ranks. At the outbreak of the Second World War, he held the rank of captain and was the commander of the 5th Destroyer Flotilla. He went on to serve in a number of different capacities and on board different Royal Navy vessels throughout the war, including the aircraft carrier HMS *Illustrious* in August 1941.

On a visit to Pearl Harbor in October 1940, Mountbatten was shocked at the Americans' lack of preparedness at their naval base, especially taking into account Japan's military manoeuvrings at the time. Seeing how badly prepared the Americans were, especially with their lack of security, he correctly predicted America would enter the war after a surprise Japanese attack on the base.

Mountbatten and his staff at Combined Operations were on a bit of a roll prior to the raid on Dieppe. On the night of 27/28 February 1942, Operation Biting, more commonly known as the Bruneval Raid, which Mountbatten and his staff had organised, took place. It was a resounding success due to the capture of a Wurzburg Radar and one of the German soldiers who helped to operate it.

A total of just 120 British airborne troops from the 1st Airborne Division landed by parachute a few miles away from the radar installation, making their way to the location on foot to carry out the attack. An interesting aspect of the men chosen to carry out the raid was that when the approval for the operation to go ahead was agreed, they had not completed their parachute training. Only two of the 1st Airborne Division's battalions were designated parachute battalions, and only one of these, the 1st Parachute Battalion, was trained and fully up to speed with their parachute training.

The division's commanding officer, Major General Frederick Browning, was opposed to the idea of giving up men from his 1st Battalion, but instead he allowed men of the 2nd Parachute Battalion, specifically C Company, to take part in the raid. All they had to do was to successfully complete their parachute training and then go straight into battle. The task of delivering the men to Bruneval was handed to Wing Commander Percy Charles Pickard of the RAF's No. 51 Squadron, and after the operation was completed, it was then down to a naval force, led by Australian Commander F.N. Cook and elements of No. 12 Commando, to evacuate the airborne troops, along with the captured radar equipment and prisoners, from the beaches at Bruneval.

The capture of the radar equipment and one of its technicians allowed the British to work out just how advanced the German system was, and how they could best get around it. There were a number of similar radar sites scattered across German-occupied Europe, but the simple reason why Bruneval was chosen as the target for Operation Biting was nothing more complicated than it was the closest to mainland Britain.

The other Commando raid that was a notable success for Mountbatten and the men of his Combined Operations unit was Operation Chariot, the attack on the heavily guarded naval dry dock at St Nazaire on the west coast of France.

What was truly remarkable about this particular raid was that those who took part in it would have known beforehand their chances of survival were minimal, and the best they could have hoped for was to have been captured. Despite knowing this, they willingly took part.

Like Bruneval, the raid at St Nazaire had a distinct purpose: to put the dry dock located there out of action. In doing so, any large German warship, such as *Tirpitz*, *Bismarck* or *Scharnhorst*, which required repairs would have to return to a German port, and in doing so would have to make their way through either the English Channel or the North Sea, putting them in danger of being attacked by both vessels of the Royal Navy and/or aircraft of the RAF.

Out of the 611 British servicemen who took part in the St Nazaire Raid, 169 were killed, while 215 were captured and became prisoners of war. Many more were wounded, and in total 60 per cent of the men who set out did not return.

Captain John Hughes-Hallett (Royal Navy)

Hughes-Hallett began his naval career as a midshipman in May 1918, in the latter stages of the First World War. He served on board the battlecruiser HMS *Lion*, the same vessel Mountbatten had served on two years earlier.

During the Norwegian Campaign of April/June 1940, he had experienced active service on board the Royal Navy heavy cruiser HMS *Devonshire*, which resulted in him being mentioned in despatches. Soon after this he started working with Mountbatten in planning Commando raids, one of which was the raid on Dieppe, for which he was the Naval Commander.

In the aftermath of the Dieppe Raid, at a meeting to look at what could be learned from the Allied defeat, Hughes-Hallett stated that if a port big enough to land all the men, vehicles and equipment required for a full-scale invasion of occupied Europe could not be identified and captured, then they should take one with them. It was an idea which had Winston Churchill's full backing.

Major General John Hamilton Roberts (Canadian Army)

After graduating from Canada's Royal Military College in Kingston in 1914, Roberts received a commission with the Royal Canadian Artillery. In 1915 he travelled to France with the Canadian Expeditionary Force and took part in the infamous Battle of the Somme the following year, where he was awarded the Military Cross for his gallantry. Whilst still in France in 1918, he was wounded and sent back to England to recover. He did not return to France and instead remained in the UK and became an artillery instructor. After the war was over, he returned to Canada and remained in the Army as a gunnery instructor.

At the outbreak of the Second World War, Roberts, who by then was a lieutenant colonel, was in charge of the 1st Field Brigade of the 1st Canadian Division, which later became the 1st Field Regiment, Royal Canadian Horse Artillery, whom he commanded in northern France. During the Battle of France in May 1940, rather than abandon his guns, put them out of action, or risk them falling into the hands of the Germans, he managed to successfully evacuate them, along with his men, at the port of Brest, in Brittany. He was the only Allied commander who managed to achieve this feat.

Having reached the rank of major general, Roberts was put in charge of the 2nd Canadian Division in April 1942. In August the same year he was appointed Commander of the Canadian Forces, who were to take part in the Dieppe Raid, although it was made clear to him that he would take no direct part in the planning of it. Despite his disappointment, he still accepted the position.

The part Roberts played in the raid was deemed to be significant enough to warrant him being awarded the French Croix de Guerre with Palm, as well as the cravat of Commander of the Legion of Honour.

On Friday, 2 October 1942 it was announced in the *London Gazette* newspaper that Roberts had been awarded the Distinguished Service Order for his 'distinguished services' during the raid on Dieppe.

> The KING has been graciously pleased to approve the following awards in recognition of gallant and distinguished services in the combined attack on Dieppe:-
> The Distinguished Service Order.
>
> Major-General John Hamilton Roberts, M.C., Commander 2nd Canadian Division, Commanding Military Forces.

Roberts was never given any further war-time operational commands and instead spent the rest of the war working in a training capacity.

On Thursday, 14 June 1945 it was announced in the *London Gazette* that Roberts had been awarded an OBE.

Air Chief Marshal Sir Trafford Leigh-Mallory (RAF)

Air Chief Marshal Sir Trafford Leigh-Mallory had begun his military career in the First World War as a private soldier in the Territorial Force battalion of the King's Regiment (Liverpool). However, on 3 October 1914 he was commissioned as a second lieutenant with the Lancashire Fusiliers.

Leigh-Mallory was, by the time of the Second Battle of Ypres (22 April–25 May 1915), serving on attachment with the South Lancashire Regiment, during which time he was wounded. On 21 June 1915, while recuperating, he was promoted to the rank of full lieutenant, an announcement of which was made in the *London Gazette* of Tuesday, 28 December 1915.

Whilst he was recovering from his wounds, he had plenty of time to sit back and contemplate both his life and his military career. Whether it was an epiphany or simply the attraction of becoming a pilot, Leigh-Malloy took the decision to join the Royal Flying Corps, which he did in January 1916 after having fully recovered from his wounds. He retained his rank of lieutenant and joined No. 7 Squadron, serving as a pilot for the rest of the war and becoming part of the newly formed RAF in April 1918.

By the beginning of the Second World War Leigh-Mallory had reached the rank of air vice marshal, and during the Battle of Britain in 1940, was in command of No.12 Group.

His involvement in the planning for Dieppe was no doubt down to his accepted knowledge and experience on the subject of Army and RAF co-operation.

Individually and collectively, this was an extremely experienced group of men, the best the British military establishment had, who should have been more than capable of planning and executing a much more successful operation than they subsequently did.

What let them down was the lack of up-to-date intelligence reports, which, if gathered correctly, would have provided the real strength of the German defensive positions in and around Dieppe, and highlighted the difficulties that would have been faced by tank crews when it came to successfully attempting to navigate their way up and away from the beaches.

The decision to use tanks in the raid had not been made because of any physical examination of the beaches, but instead was achieved by members of the planning team simply scanning through holiday photographs submitted by members of the British public who had holidayed in the area in the years leading up to the war. Aerial reconnaissance missions were also undertaken by the RAF, but despite this, some of the German defensive gun positions on the cliffs above Dieppe had been missed. The other important aspect which had apparently also been missed was that the beaches at Dieppe were made of stones and pebbles, not sand, which not only made it difficult for heavy vehicles such as tanks to grip, but also for the troops to run across at any great speed.

In the original plan for Operation Rutter, which is covered in more detail in Chapter 2, and which would later become Operation Jubilee, the intelligence reports indicated that Dieppe was not heavily defended and that the local beaches were suitable for the landing of heavy vehicles. On 19 August 1942, the day of the raid, the use of this incorrect intelligence undoubtedly cost many lives, which was ultimately avoidable.

This aspect of the raid is hard to fathom because covert surveillance of beaches in enemy-controlled areas had already been thought of and carried out.

In fairness to the planners of Operation Jubilee, such measures had only been used once prior to the raid on Dieppe. This particular occasion was in March 1941, during the planning for the proposed raid on the Italian-occupied Greek island of Rhodes, Operation Cordite, an operation which never subsequently took place. The operation consisted of two men, Lieutenant Herbert Nigel Clogstoun-Willmott of the Royal Navy, and Captain Roger 'Jumbo' James Allen Courtney, of the British Army, carrying out surveillance on the island to see what useful information they could glean before any such raid took place. What made their task even more remarkable was that the two men alighted from a submarine approximately half a mile out to sea and swam to the beach to carry out their reconnaissance. When they were finished, they had to swim the same distance back out to sea to rendezvous with the submarine that had dropped them off.

By the end of 1941, Combined Operations had developed the work carried out at Rhodes by Clogstoun-Willmott and Courtney, and come up with the Combined Operations Assault Pilotage Parties, more commonly referred to as COAPPs. The men who served in this unit were drawn from the Royal Navy, Royal Marines, the Corps of Royal Engineers and the Special Boat Service. These were all extremely brave young men who risked their lives landing on enemy beaches to establish if they were suitable as proposed landing sites for amphibious landings of men and equipment. These clandestine reconnaissance missions, often carried out in the dead of night, were invaluable because they provided the planners of such raids with first-hand, up-to-date information about what those taking part in the mission would potentially have to contend with; information which could not be gleaned by sifting through any number of photographs.

These visits, carried out by teams of two men in a canoe, allowed for accurate information to be obtained on matters such as tides, currents, water depths, and whether there were any obvious underwater hazards, such as rocks, sandbanks or, more importantly, if the waters closer to the beach were mined. The composition of the beach could clearly be established and samples of it obtained, if necessary, so as to establish which if any military vehicles would be able to land on it.

The two-man COAPP teams would be delivered close to their destinations by submarines and would make the final part of their journey to the beach by canoe.

Another aspect of the build-up to the raid on Dieppe is what has become known as the First Moscow Conference, which had the codename of 'Bracelet'. This meeting saw Winston Churchill and Joseph Stalin, joined by Averell Harriman, a representative of President Roosevelt, meet between 12 and 17 August 1942. The conference finished just two days before the raid on Dieppe took place. There were two main topics of conversation: the North Africa Campaign and the possibility of the opening of another front, somewhere in northern France, with the latter understandably being of more urgent concern to Stalin than it was to either Churchill or Roosevelt.

In an effort to aid his country's fight against Nazi Germany, Stalin demanded the immediate opening of the aforementioned second front, but to no avail. Churchill was having none of it, and politely, but firmly, explained that such actions were simply not possible at that time. He made the point of emphasising that it was not because he did not want to, but simply because neither the British nor the Americans had sufficient manpower or equipment to successfully undertake such a commitment.

The timing of the two events is nothing more than coincidental, as there is no way that Churchill could have returned from the conference and then arranged for the raid on Dieppe to take place. The planning and organisation of the operation had clearly been in place for some time, and certainly before 12 August 1942.

It is interesting to note that Churchill made absolutely no mention to Stalin of the raid that was about to take place at Dieppe, and Stalin's reaction to the subsequent raid is not recorded. When he did find out, it can only be assumed that he made enquiries with British authorities to discover whether Dieppe was either a raid or a failed attempt at an invasion of occupied Europe. Even if it had been the latter of the two options, such a failing would never have been admitted.

CHAPTER TWO

Operation Rutter

In essence, Operation Rutter was the original version of Operation Jubilee, but it had to be cancelled at the very last minute, mainly due to the inclement weather which prevailed across the English Channel on 7 July 1942, the date when it was originally due to have taken place.

Rutter was to have been a combined operation featuring aircraft from the RAF's Bomber Command and vessels from the Royal Navy, who would collectively bombard German defensive positions in and the areas immediately surrounding Dieppe. In addition to this, airborne troops were to be parachuted onto the cliffs overlooking the beaches, where the troops and tanks that would comprise the bulk of the raiding party would be brought ashore by landing craft.

Regardless of the name Rutter or Jubilee, a raid such as this was always going to take place, primarily because if something of this size could not be properly planned and actioned, then there were always going to be grave concerns about the viability of a full-scale invasion force crossing the English Channel, landing on the French coast, gaining a foothold on the beaches, and then fighting their way inland to defeat Nazi Germany and finally put an end to the war.

It was felt by Churchill, his government and other Allied nations that it was important to show Stalin there was a desire to assist him in his country's fight against Germany. However, there was no real empathy or love for Stalin or the Russian people. It was more a policy of self-preservation. If Britain and her allies could not convince Stalin that they saw him as an equal, and that they needed him to be patient, then there was a real risk that he would look to end the war with Germany by signing a peace agreement with Hitler.

In July 1941, following Hitler's invasion of Russia the previous month, Stalin offered to cede the Baltic states and Ukraine to Germany, and less than a year later, in May 1942, he also offered to add Belarus as well. What made such a deal even more of a possibility was the fact that Stalin did not really trust Britain or the United States, especially when it came to what their real intentions for the outcome of the war actually were. For all Stalin knew, the West could simply have been biding its time while waiting for the USSR and Germany to destroy each other beyond a state of repair, and then simply move in to pick up the pieces of what was left.

It was potentially a massive problem for Britain and the USA if Stalin made peace with Hitler. With no war to fight in the East, Hitler would have been free to send all his troops deployed there to bolster the eastern side of his newly acquired empire. Figures are not exact, but Soviet sources estimate that between 1941 and 1945, more than 4 million German troops were killed, and a further 3 million were captured and became POWs.

Imagine how difficult it would have been for the Allies to have invaded German-occupied Europe if just half of those men who had been fighting on the Eastern Front had been available, in addition to those already there, to defend the Normandy beaches in June 1944. Even if successful, which is unlikely, the Allied losses in both men and equipment would have been astronomical, and the war would have then continued for many more years and resulted in thousands more Allied casualties.

When taking in to account Soviet losses, there is a clearer picture of how close a peace treaty between Stalin and German actually was. The Battle of Stalingrad, which took place between 23 August 1942 and 2 February 1943, began just four days after the raid on Dieppe. Even though Stalingrad resulted in a Soviet victory, their losses were colossal: 1,129,619 casualties, which included 950,000 combat casualties, of which 478,741 were killed or missing and 650,878 who were either wounded or sick. If the raid on Dieppe had been the actual second front that Stalin had demanded, then Soviet casualties would have been greatly reduced.

The Dieppe Raid was seen by Churchill as an opportunity to increase the morale of the British public after they had already experienced a number of defeats and setbacks up to that point in the war. A cross-section of the British public also supported the introduction of a second front because they believed it was the right and proper thing to do in support of the people of the Soviet Union.

From a military perspective, there was a belief that for any invasion of occupied Europe to be successful, a French port would need to be captured so that support vessels carrying both men and equipment could be landed for an invasion to begin in earnest. But it was unclear just how well defended French ports were. The concern was whether Allied forces could gain control of a port before German defenders could either destroy it or have sufficient men and equipment in place to successfully defend it against a larger invading Allied force.

Another unknown was the viability of keeping a large invading force from making its way across the English Channel, unseen by German forces. The element of surprise was paramount to the success of such a venture. If discovered before the final run in to the beach or harbour, any casualties would likely be greatly increased as not only would shore batteries open fire, but aircraft and naval vessels could be deployed as well.

Operation Rutter was different from its later incarnation of Jubilee in so far as the plan was to use airborne troops to deal with German defences covering the approaches to the port at Dieppe. Then, after RAF bombers and Royal Navy vessels had bombarded German artillery positions on the cliffs overlooking the main landing beaches, gliders would land on the cliffs and the troops they were carrying would then disembark and finish off any German troops at the gun batteries who might still be alive.

Having made it ashore, the raiding troops and tanks were to make their way off the beaches, out of the port area, and head inland to the outskirts of the town. The purpose then was to hold any and all enemy counterattacks until the signal was given to withdraw. They would then make their way back to the beaches, re-embark the landing craft that had dropped them off, and then make their way back across the English Channel to safety.

The main raiding force would come from the 2nd Canadian Infantry Division, which included the Royal Regiment of Canada, the Royal Hamilton Light infantry, the Essex Scottish Regiment, Les Fusiliers Mont-Royal, the Queen's Own Cameron Highlanders of Canada, the South Saskatchewan Regiment, and the 14th Army Tank Regiment (the Calgary Regiment Tank).

The Canadian high command had pushed for Canadian forces to play a part in the raid, but the price they would pay for the 'privilege' would haunt them for ever more.

Canadian troops had first arrived in England in December 1939 in the form of men of the 1st Canadian Infantry Division, and within a couple months their numbers had risen to nearly 25,000. They became part of the British South-Eastern Command and were tasked with defending England's southern coastline between Newhaven and Worthing, Sussex, but by the end of 1941, and with the war stretching in to its third year, Canadian troops as well as their political leaders wanted to be more involved in the actual fighting of the war. When the idea for the raid on Dieppe was first voiced, it was decided that this was the opportunity for the Canadians to be given their chance.

One of the lingering questions about the raid has always been whether the Canadians were up to the task they had been set. This is not meant as a slur, or to question the passion, drive or professionalism of the Canadian forces who took part in the raid, but rather a look at the standard and quality of the training they were given in preparation for what was to come.

For many of the senior Canadian officers, their only previous fighting experience had been as junior officers during the years of the First World War more than twenty years earlier. Since then, military tactics had changed dramatically, meaning that a young, dynamic and competent officer who had fought and seen action during the predominantly trench warfare style fighting which then prevailed, had little or no understanding of the pressures and requirements of modern warfare, as was needed in 1942.

The 2nd Canadian Infantry Division spent April, May and June training and practising for the raid on the Isle of

Wight. The training primarily involved learning how to get on and off naval war ships and landing craft. Transferring from a war ship onto a landing craft, or from a landing craft on to a beach, was not for the feint hearted. If this aspect of the training was not mastered, there would be no major landing on an enemy-controlled beach. It was an important part of the exercise, just as it would be in the actual operation. The men would also have trained for the roles they were to undertake once they had landed. Each unit would have been allocated a task, which formed part of the overall plan. How compantently these tasks were carried out went a long way to determining the outcome of the operation. With the training complete, the Canadian forces would next take part in two exercises on the Dorset coastline, near the town of Bridport.

The first full-scale exercise was known as Exercise Yukon and took place in June 1942, with Operation Rutter scheduled to take place in the first week of July. The exercise involved approximately 4,000 Canadian troops, who landed, along with several tanks, on the beaches spread out between West Bay and Bridport along the Dorset coastline. Having made it ashore, the troops were then tasked with making their way nearly 3 miles inland to the village of Bradpole. From there, they made their way back to beaches and re-embarked on the waiting landing craft.

Whilst the exercise was underway, the civilian population of West Bay were temporarily moved out of their homes for safety and security reasons, but those further inland were not. At Bradpole, for example, the students of St James's Secretarial College, which continues in the same capacity today, were still hard at work with their studies. As the pupils sat in the grounds of the college enjoying the excellent summer weather, they were suddenly distracted by large numbers of Canadian soldiers making their way through the college's garden. Having been given no prior warning of the soldiers' arrival, there were certainly one or two surprised faces amongst the young female students.

The exercise was far from being a success, in part because of the inclement coastal weather, but in the main because of how poorly organised the exercise had been.

At this time, the General Officer Commanding of Britain's South-Eastern Command was Lieutenant General Bernard Montgomery. Having watched the exercise, he was so unimpressed with what he saw that he ordered the exercise to be repeated, which it was eleven days later. On that occasion, Montgomery was sufficiently happy with what he had seen for Operation Rutter to go ahead. It would appear that if he had not intervened as he did after the end of the first running of the exercise, many more Canadians would have been killed when the raid on Dieppe eventually took place.

Another downside of such events is that they require the concentration of large numbers of men, equipment and vessels in a particular area, which can be extremely difficult to keep secret.

July 1942 was no exception to this rule, because just after 06.00 on 7 July, Allied vessels at anchor in the waters of the Solent, off the Isle of Wight, fully laden with Canadian soldiers who had been fully briefed, were awaiting to set sail for Dieppe when they were attacked by German aircraft. Two of the vessels, HMS *Princess Astrid* and HMS *Princess Josephine Charlotte*, were struck in the attack. Both of these Belgian-owned ships had been passenger vessels before the war, plying their trade backwards and forwards across the English Channel between Belgium and England. Following the outbreak of the war, they had been requisitioned and converted into troop landing ships.

Luckily, the damage to either vessel was not serious. In fact, as far as the *Princess Astrid* was concerned, there was hardly any damage at all. A bomb landed on C deck but had struck the upper structure of a landing vessel located on the side of the ship, before bouncing into the water and exploding.

Whether the German pilots realised the significance of what they had encountered when they carried out their attack is unclear, but fortunately for the Canadian and British forces on board those vessels, the German aircraft did not return.

The Commonwealth War Graves Commission lists the names of two Canadian soldiers who were killed in England on 7 July 1942. Lance Corporal Antonio Langlais of Le Régiment de la Chaudière, and Warrant Officer Class II William Hartwell Showler, of the Canadian Army Corps of Military Staff Clerks.

HMS *Princess Astrid* would later take part in the raid on Dieppe by conveying Canadian troops to what had been designated as 'Blue Beach', having left Portsmouth harbour just before 21.00 on 18 August 1942, where the plan was to set out from five ports on the south coast of England, (Southampton, Portsmouth, Newhaven, Shoreham and Gosport), before making its way across the English Channel to Dieppe.

When it was decided that Operation Rutter should not be discarded but instead 'revamped' as Operation Jubilee, Montgomery was against the idea because of concerns over potential security breaches. The Canadian soldiers who had been preparing to set sail for Dieppe had all been fully briefed about the raid and the individual parts they were to play in it. If these men were then stood down, even only temporarily, and were then allowed out for just a matter of hours, it would only take one man to speak out, which was likely if alcohol was involved, and such careless talk could result in the unnecessary deaths of hundreds of men.

Although Operation Rutter never took place and was subsequently replaced by Jubilee, it would not be unrealistic to assume that the same considerations were part of the aftermath of the latter operation. That being the case, it shows there was a desire to create a positive relationship between Britain and the Soviet leader, Joseph Stalin, and that there was a direct link between the raid on Dieppe and a desire to impress and appease the Russians sufficiently enough to keep them on the Allies' side.

A letter dated 30 June 1942 sent by Mountbatten to Rear Admiral H.T. Baillie-Grohman, Major General J.H. Roberts, and Air Vice Marshal Leigh-Malloy was marked as MOST SECRET. It highlighted this point and came under the heading of:

Operation "Rutter" – Messages to Russia

(1). The Ministry of Information, anxious to promote good relations between Great Britain and Russia, have invited my co-operation in helping to achieve this desirable object.

(2). The Ministry point out that the treaty recently signed by the British and Soviet Governments has aroused intense interest in Russia, where the people have never been more susceptible than they are now to a development of the existing friendship between our two countries.

(3). One of the requests made by the Ministry is that messages should be sent from Force Commanders on their return from a Combined Operation to their opposite numbers on whichever part of the Russian front is then prominent in the news. This form of propaganda, I am assured, is always extremely popular with the Russians, and is calculated to have beneficial results in the cause of Anglo-Soviet good relations.

(4). I should be grateful, therefore, if you would each be good enough to prepare such a message immediately after "Rutter", or delegate an officer who took part in the operation to do so, for submission to my Headquarters.

(5). I am instructing Captain David Astor, R.M., an officer in my Public Relations section, to approach the Naval and Military Force Commanders on their return from the operation to assist them in this matter. Could Air-Vice Marshal Leigh-Mallory arrange for a message to be sent to this Headquarters from himself or one of his officers. This could be done through his P.R.O at No. 11 Group, who might conveniently make contact with the S.P.R.O. at my Headquarters after the operation.

(6). I will arrange for the messages to be given to the Ministry of Information for despatch to Russia as soon as possible after the action, and I shall much appreciate your collaboration in a project to which the Ministry attach considerable importance.

Louis Mountbatten
Chief of Combined Operations

P.S. I am making arrangements to ensure that these messages will not be published in the English Press.

The treaty referred to in point (2) was the Anglo-Soviet Treaty, signed in London on 26 May 1942 by the British Foreign Secretary, Sir Anthony Eden, and his Soviet counterpart, Vyacheslav Molotov. This was a military and political alliance, with the military aspect lasting until the end of the Second World War, and the political aspect for twenty years from the date it was signed.

CHAPTER THREE

The Raid on Dieppe

For the Canadian soldiers, Dieppe was a major turning point of the war as despite having been in England for two years, they had not been anywhere near a battlefield. Dieppe would finally be their opportunity to take part in the fighting and show their British and Allied counterparts exactly what they were capable of.

A total of 4,963 Canadian officers and men took part in the raid. By the time it was over, 907 of them had been killed, 2,460 had been wounded, while those captured and taken as POWs numbered 1,946. The more seriously wounded men received medical treatment at nearby hospitals, whilst all other POWs were sent into captivity to a number of different camps located throughout Germany.

To have a complete understanding of the raid on Dieppe, and to consider what part it played in the war, it is important to start at the very beginning, and look at what took place in more detail.

Planning Phase

The man ultimately in charge of the operation was Admiral Louis Mountbatten, head of the Combined Operations Headquarters.

All such operations had at their core different elements such as manpower, equipment, communications, transport, object, method and intention.

To a large extent the operation was based on intelligence reports which had been gathered in the build-up and planning stages. Unfortunately for the Allied forces taking part in the raid, all the reports said that Dieppe was not heavily defended and that the identified beaches were suitable for the landing of both troops and heavy military vehicles.

With the planning of the operation underway, the objectives were allocated to different sections of the raiding party, which included destroying enemy defences in and around the immediate area of Dieppe. At the nearby town of St Aubin was a small airfield, only opened in 1934, but which before the war had seen significant levels of air traffic, with tourists visiting the area for their holidays. The airfield needed knocking out, including its communications ability, to prevent the possibility of German re-enforcements landing and bolstering the defensive positions.

Targets such as power and radar stations, harbour facilities, railways and fuel dumps were to be attacked and destroyed or put out of action. A number of sea-going barges, which the Germans had intended to use for their planned, then cancelled, invasion of Britain, were laid up at Dieppe. The plan was to recover these for future use by the Allies, possibly with the future Normandy landings in mind.

Another target were the local German headquarters at the castle of Aques-la-Bataille, which was also an ammunition depot protected by anti-aircraft guns. It was believed that certain sensitive military documents were held at the castle, although exactly what information these documents contained was not revealed.

As with all such raids, the capture of enemy personnel was also high on the agenda. Information they potentially possessed had the capacity to be of use to the Allied war effort, even if it was only down to being able to identify what enemy units were stationed in the vicinity of the raid.

The main point of the raid was to land troops at Dieppe, secure the town, its harbour and the surrounding area, hold it for a period of time whilst fending off enemy counterattacks, and to safely re-embark back to England. In the original plan for Operation Rutter, the plan also called for the use of airborne troops, a naval bombardment and troops brought in by glider aircraft.

By the time Rutter had become Operation Jubilee, the latter three elements had been dropped from the planning. The naval bombardment was dismissed because of the concern that this would dramatically increase the number of French civilians who might be killed. The Royal Navy also had concerns that they might make easy targets for the German Luftwaffe if they took to the skies in sufficient numbers.

As for the airborne and glider elements, there were two particular concerns: the potential for inclement weather would greatly hinder their effectiveness, and if the element of surprise was therefore lost early in the operation, this could result in a mass slaughter of the troops involved before they had even landed. Aerial bombing of the town was also dropped from the plan for the same weather-related reasons.

Nevertheless, the RAF still played an active part in the raid. The man in charge was Air Vice Marshal Trafford Leigh-Mallory, the commander of 11 Group Fighter Command who were stationed at RAF Uxbridge, which was also his headquarters for the raid. Part of his strategy was to try to force the Luftwaffe into a large-scale aerial fight in the skies over Dieppe and inflict a major defeat upon them.

What made Leigh-Mallory an excellent choice for involvement in the raid on Dieppe was his knowledge and experience in the co-operation between the Army and RAF. Indeed, in 1930 he had given a lecture at the Royal Unites Services Institute on the subject of air co-operation with mechanised forces.

During the Battle of Britain, Leigh-Mallory was in command of No. 12 Group, whose role it was to protect RAF airfields in the south-east of England. Along with Douglas Bader, he had devised an aerial fighting tactic known as Big Wing, which in essence meant meeting incoming Luftwaffe bombing raids in strength with a wing shaped formation of up to five squadrons.

By the time of the raid on Dieppe, Leigh-Mallory would deploy a total of fifty-six fighter squadrons, including Spitfires, Hurricanes and Typhoons, which would make up the fighter element of the raid. There were also four squadrons of American P-51 Mustang Mk 1 aircraft that formed the reconnaissance aspect, as well as five squadrons of bomber aircraft, whose main function was to drop smoke across the beaches and to bomb designated targets in support of the troops who had made it off the beaches and into Dieppe.

Elements of No. 88, No. 107, and No. 266 squadrons, who were part of No. 2 Group of Bomber Command, were also involved in the operation. Douglas A-20 Havoc medium bombers, an American made multi-purpose aircraft, were in service with both No. 88 and 107 squadrons. In August 1942, the two squadrons, who were based in the east of England, each sent a number of their aircraft to RAF Ford in West Sussex, which was the setting off point for most of the aircraft. The exception being No. 266 Squadron, who took off from their base at RAF Thruxton in Hampshire, with their job being to drop the smoke screen across the beaches and cliffs at Dieppe.

The raid also included other RAF stations such as the ones at Cheadle and Kingston, which were known as "Y" stations, part of the UK's network of signals and intelligence collection sites who intercepted German radio transmissions. Anything that was then deemed of relevance to the raiding party was passed on to HMS *Calpe*, the designated headquarters ship for the raid, who were in contact with the bomber aircraft and their crews.

The Raid on Dieppe

The aircraft and vessels which took part in the Dieppe Raid included 74 squadrons of aircraft from the RAF, as well as 237 ships and landing craft from the Royal Navy. The latter left from a number of different ports situated along the south coast of England.

With so many naval vessels, which included eight destroyers, taking part in the raid, it would have been impractical to have even contemplated all those ships manoeuvring in and around just one port. There is also every chance that such a large formation would have come to the notice of German spies, which could have resulted in the Luftwaffe carrying out a surprise attack with potentially catastrophic losses in both ships and men. Such information would have also alerted the German defensive forces to the likelihood of an imminent raid somewhere along the west coast of France.

The following Allied units took part in the raid:

    The South Saskatchewan Regiment
    The Royal Hamilton Light Infantry
    The Essex Scottish Regiment
    No. 3 Commando
    The Royal Regiment of Canada
    14th Tank Battalion (Calgary Tanks)
    Royal Marines
    The Queen's Own Cameron Highlanders of Canada
    No. 4 Commando
    Les Fusiliers Mont-Royal
    1st Ranger Battalion
    No. 10 Commando
    No. 30 Commando
    No. 40 Commando

On the evening of 18 August 1942, just after dark, the raiding party set sail for Dieppe. In keeping with the time of year it was a warm and the moon was clearly visible high up in the sky. Anchors were raised, engines started, as all the ships gradually made their way out into the English Channel, preceded by Royal Navy minesweepers out of Newhaven, who cleared a path for the raiding party to follow. Everything was carried out with the military precision to be expected of such an occasion.

The First Sea Lord, Sir Dudley Pound, found himself facing somewhat of a dilemma. Mountbatten had personally asked him to send one of his battleships as part of the raid because of the greater fire power it would be able to provide. As part of its armoury it was not uncommon for such vessels to have a battery of sixteen 4.1-inch (105-mm) guns, which was a formidable arsenal for any raiding party to have at their disposal.

Sir Dudley was concerned with deploying one of his capital ships to locations where the RAF did not have control of the skies, feeling that to do so would place the vessel in unnecessary danger from German aerial attack.

Part of any war is about learning from mistakes which have already taken place. On 10 December 1941, off the Malaysian coastline at Kuantan, the Royal Navy battleship HMS *Prince of Wales* was attacked and sunk by Japanese Mitsubishi G3M bomber aircraft, some of which were armed with torpedoes. A total of 327 crew members of the *Prince of Wales* were killed in the attack. One of the major contributing factors for the loss was the total absence of any air cover.

Instead, all Sir Dudley was prepared to send on the raid were six Hunt-class destroyers, each of which had a total of six 4-inch (102-mm) guns.

As the raiding party made their way towards the beaches, ahead were their allocated landing points, which had been colour coded from left to right:

Yellow Beach – Berneval
Blue Beach – Puys
Red Beach – Dieppe
White Beach – Dieppe
Green Beach – Pourville
Orange Beach – Varengville

Yellow Beach

No. 3 Commando were tasked with knocking out the German defensive coastal battery, which had been given the somewhat ironic 'nickname' of Goebbels, located about half a mile inland above the cliffs at Berneval-le-Grand. This had to be achieved prior to the arrival of the main raiding party, who would be landing at Dieppe just 4 miles away. Failure to achieve this part of the operation would potentially result in hundreds more Allied casualties, because if the battery's seven guns were allowed to fire at will in the general direction of the Canadian forces carrying out the assault, it could well have resulted in a bloodbath.

As was often the way with such operations, things did not always go according to plan. This was certainly the case for the men of No. 3 Commando at Dieppe. At 03.48, while on their way into their designated beaches, the twenty-three landing craft came across a German coastal convoy consisting of a German merchant vessel carrying much needed fuel, and a number of armed trawlers. Although the enemy vessels had been located and identified by the RAF's early warning "Chain Home" radar stations on the coast of West Sussex, this information was not transmitted to the vessels taking part in the raid. There was no specific reason ever given for this. Perhaps the British radar stations were not aware that such an operation was taking place, or if they were, they were unclear as to the location of British surface vessels in relation to the German convoy. This convoy had initially been detected at 21.30 on 18 August, and the meeting with No.3 Commando did not take place until 03.48 the following day.

As if the contact with the German vessels was not bad enough, the two destroyers tasked with protecting the landing craft, HMS *Brocklesby*, which was part of the 15th Destroyer Flotilla based at Portsmouth, and ORP *Slazak*, of the Polish navy, misunderstood where the artillery fire had come from. For some unknown reason, the captains of these two vessels did not appear to have realised what had happened and had assumed that the incoming fire being sustained by the landing craft came from shore batteries and not the German ships. Thankfully, the German trawlers did not understand the true significance of the Allied vessels they had come across, but that did not prevent them from opening fire, quite possibly in the belief that they were about to be attacked.

Of the twenty-three landing craft the Commandos were aboard, only seven of them made it to their intended beaches at Berneval. Eight were damaged in the contact with the German convoy and had to return to England, a further four were sunk, whilst four others had already returned home due to engine trouble.

Commandos from six of the landing craft made it onto their designated beach, code named Yellow I, but were immediately met by strong German resistance. Now stranded, they were unable to move any further forward because of the intense German fire being rained down upon them, while any attempt to make it back to their landing craft would have meant certain death. With no other options available, they surrendered. Their intended target had been to knock out the Goebbels battery situated near Berneval-le-Grand, which was about half a mile inland and towards the top of a steep cliff.

The two Brigade headquarter sections did not fare much better. One of them came under such heavy fire that the craft they were on board never made it ashore and none of the men made it to the beach as they were all killed before doing so. The vessel that the other section had been on board had been so badly damaged by enemy gunfire, that even before they made it to the beach they had already sustained heavy casualties. Only one officer eventually made it ashore, only for the men to then spend the rest of the raid pinned down by enemy fire on the beach. By the end of the raid, only fifteen of those who had made it ashore were still alive.

The eighteen Commandos on board the seventh landing craft, which landed on the other end of the same beach (Yellow II) had more luck when they came ashore. They managed to get off the beach and although they were unable to knock out their target (the battery at Berneval), they were able to carry out a sustained attack on it long enough to prevent it from opening fire on any of the other landing craft that were making their way to the beaches.

As the fighting continued, the Germans managed to bring reinforcements to the area immediately around the battery the Commandos were attacking. It soon became apparent they were not going to get any further with their attack in the face of a now greatly enlarged enemy force, so they made the reluctant decision to withdraw whilst still in a position to do so.

The names of the members of No. 3 Commando who were killed in the raid are included in Appendix B.

Besides men, the plan included landing a number of tanks on the beaches at Dieppe, but this proved much harder to achieve than had been anticipated. The tanks were on board three Landing Craft, Tanks, more commonly referred to as LCTs. There were twenty-nine of them in total. The LCTs made it all the way to the beach meaning that the tanks were able to land on 'dry land' rather than have to fight their way through the breaking waves of the sea. There was a problem, however, as the Germans had anticipated such an eventuality and had built an anti-tank ditch across the entire width of the beach, meaning that the potential effectiveness which the tanks provided had been greatly nullified almost immediately.

One of the tanks somehow managed to reach the promenade road by making its way to the extreme east of the beach, close to the harbour jetty, but no sooner had it done this than it came under attack from German defences high up on the cliffs. Another tank also managed to make it off the beach and up onto the promenade by making its way to the extreme west end of the beach, but it also came under heavy enemy fire. Both tanks were then limited as to what to do next as they were prevented from entering the town by substantial German roadblocks, leaving the tanks only capable of firing at German defensive positions from their limited position on the promenade.

Approximately eighteen of the tanks had been disabled by enemy fire knocking out their tracks. None of the tanks which had landed was evacuated, but this was more because nearly all of the LCTs which landed them on the beach had been sunk by German artillery or mortar fire. The other problem which had arisen was that of communications. Despite the tank commanders being in touch with each other via radio, there was no communication between the tanks and the infantry units.

F Battalion had initially been held back in reserve for the 'just in case' scenario part of the raid, but their desire to be part of the fighting was granted early on when they were sent forward to assist C and D battalions fight their way into Dieppe.

A number of men from F Battalion had already been wounded or killed before they had even reached the beach, as the vessels they were on board had sustained a number of hits and either been badly damaged or sunk by German guns . For the men of F Battalion who did make it ashore, large numbers were cut down by withering German machine gun fire almost as soon as they disembarked. Those who had survived, meanwhile, found themselves trapped on the beach.

Blue Beach

The Royal Regiment of Canada, supported by three platoons from The Black Watch (Royal Highland Regiment) of Canada, equipped with mortars and machine guns, had possibly the most unusual and difficult of tasks as they had to land on a small beach at Puys, to the west of Dieppe. The two regiments had been tasked with destroying the German machine gun positions and artillery batteries, which were in place to provide defensive cover for the beaches at Dieppe.

One of the immediate problems they encountered was that there was no direct way to exit the beach. The best they could do was to try to reach the seawall at the top end of the beach, thus finding themselves some kind of cover that would protect them from the merciless machine gun fire and mortar shells. Unfortunately, the sheer cliff face at the end of the beach was much taller than had been anticipated.

Sadly, for those men due to land on what had been designated as Blue Beach, any element of surprise which they had in their favour had been completely lost by the sound of the gunfire and commotion coming from slightly further along the beach at Berneval, where the men of No. 3 Commando had come ashore.

Part of the plan at Blue Beach was for smoke cannisters to be dropped to provide the large raiding party with an element of cover, which if nothing else would give them valuable extra seconds to come ashore safely and gain some kind of foothold on the beach. It was a good idea, but the flaw in the plan was that the units coming ashore at Blue Beach had been delayed by more than 20 minutes, meaning that by the time the landing craft they were in actually hit the beach, at just after 05.00, the smoke had already dissipated and dawn had broken. Already alerted by the gunfire coming from their right-hand side, any doubt for the German defenders as to what was happening was confirmed by the presence of the heavy smoke dropped on the beach in front of them.

The added problem here was that the Germans defending this location had an obvious advantage over the Canadians tasked with landing there. The main German defences in the area were set up specifically to deal with an amphibious attack, meaning all their artillery batteries and machine gun nests were facing down onto the beach and out to sea.

Of the 556 men of the Royal Regiment of Canada who landed on the beach at Puys, only 81 were rescued. The Commonwealth War Graves Commission lists 211 members of the Royal Regiment of Canada as being killed on 19 August, meaning that if those figures are correct, 264 men were captured. This figure does not, of course, include those who subsequently died of wounds sustained that same day.

Meanwhile, only two members of the Black Watch are recorded to have been killed during the landings on Blue Beach. However, records held by the Canadian government state that the Black Watch incurred four fatal casualties during the raid.

If Operation Rutter had gone ahead as planned, many of the German defensive positions high up on the cliffs overlooking the beaches would have been taken out via a naval bombardment and aerial attack by RAF aircraft from Bomber Command. This would have then been followed by British parachutists tasked with taking out any German defenders who had survived. However, as we have seen, when Operation Rutter became Operation Jubilee, the preliminary naval and aerial bombardments were removed.

Red & White Beaches

The units selected for the beaches designated as 'Red' and 'White', towards the centre of Dieppe, were the Royal Hamilton Light Infantry, the Essex Scottish, the Fusiliers Mont-Royal, Royal Marines A Commando, and the 14th Canadian Army Tank Regiment (Calgary Tanks). The first of the units came ashore at just before 03.00.

The tactics were quite simple: the men of the Essex Scottish and the Royal Hamilton Light Infantry would lead the main assault, with the immediate assistance of tanks from the 14th Canadian Army Tank Regiment. However, the two groups did not arrive at the same time, which left the infantry vulnerable. Once the men of the Royal Hamilton Light Infantry and the Essex Scottish were on the beach, they had no choice but to begin their attack. Otherwise, they would have just been sitting ducks, stood on a beach that afforded them absolutely no cover or protection.

With the original outline of Operation Rutter having been changed so drastically, the decision for these units to carry out a frontal assault could be described as almost suicidal, especially for men who had never been in battle before. For many, the baptism of fire they were greeted with at Dieppe would be the first and last time they would experience it. Those landing on Red and White beaches had to deal with the additional threat from numerous German machine gunners positioned in the upper stories of buildings, immediately overlooking the seafront and harbour area.

A total of twenty-seven Churchill tanks, a mixture of Mark I, IIs and IIIs that were seeing combat for the first time at Dieppe, managed to make it onto the beach. Of these, fifteen made it across and off the beach and headed towards the centre of town, but because of defensive obstacles that blocked their advance, they were left with no option but to return to the beach, making themselves easy targets in the process. Nevertheless, despite being either hit by German artillery or floundering on the beach's large shingle, they were able to offer effective covering fire for the retreating Canadian forces at the end of the raid.

One of the LCTs, with three Churchill tanks on board, had left from Newhaven and arrived at its designated drop off point at 06.00. As soon as the vehicles hit the beach, however, they almost immediately came under attack from German artillery and were struck by three rounds in quick succession, partly setting the landing craft on fire. After helping to load the wounded onto another vessel, the remaining crew of the LCT were left stranded on the beach with very little to hide behind for cover. Not long after, these men were left with no other option than to surrender. For them, the fighting was over almost as soon as it had begun.

It is unclear if there was ever any intention to bring the Churchill tanks back to the UK after the raid. Even if things had gone better for the Allied forces, the practicalities and time it would have taken to manoeuvre just one cumbersome and slow-moving tank across the beach and attempt to re-embark it onto a landing craft bobbing up and down in the unpredictable waves at Dieppe would have made it an extremely difficult task. To attempt this in a training capacity would have been difficult enough, without the added element of German ground and air forces attacking with everything they had at their disposal.

Green Beach

The 1st Battalion, South Saskatchewan Regiment, along with the Queen's Own Cameron Highlanders of Canada, came ashore at Pourville, west of Dieppe, at just before 05.00.

There was an immediate problem with the landing because despite the fact that nearly all the men managed to disembark from their respective landing craft before the Germans were aware of their presence, a number of the craft landed in the wrong location. Instead of landing to the east of the River Scie, a number of them ended up on the west side of the river, meaning that when they made it off the beach, they then had to cross over a heavily guarded bridge to ensure they were on the correct side to reach their intended target; the Hindenburg artillery battery, located in the hills to the east and west of the port. This, along with the fact that German reinforcements quickly flooded the area with machine gun and mortar fire, greatly affected the men of both regiments from being able to successfully achieve their parts of the raid.

Canadian dead and wounded lay across the bridge, having been cut down in their attempts to cross it. This quickly became one of those moments in a battle when extraordinary bravery was required if the remaining Canadians were to move forward. It was a classic Catch-22 situation, in that there was as much chance of them being killed if they remained on the far side of the bridge than if they tried to cross it. As the commanding officer of the South Saskatchewan Regiment, Lieutenant Colonel Charles Merritt was a decisive man who liked to lead from the front. He knew that the longer he and his men lingered on the wrong side of the bridge, the more dangerous their situation would become.

What possessed Merrit to do what he did next, only he will know. Without any warning to the remainder of his men, he stood up, took off his steel helmet, waved it in the air above his head and beckoned his men to follow him in an improvised charge across the bridge, calling out as he ran, 'Come on over, there's nothing to it'. This not only took his men by surprise, but the Germans on the other side of the bridge as well. It was not long before Merritt and his remaining men made it to the far bank. But being low in ammunition, especially mortars, and unable to communicate via radio to the destroyers out to sea to call in supporting fire, his attacking options were greatly hampered. The route to his intended targets was severely hindered because of the presence of a number of defensive concrete pillboxes. Rather than stand his ground, Merritt once again went on the offensive and led attacks on each of the pillboxes, knocking them out of action, one at a time.

Merritt and his men had moved forward as far as they could, and all that was left for them to do was to hold their position until it was time to retreat back to the beaches. The main importance for him was to keep in touch with all his section positions so that everybody was up to speed with the current situation. He did this to such a degree that when his runner was killed by German fire, he took the role upon himself.

When the time came to withdraw, Merritt, along with a number of his officers and men, held a rearguard position close to the seawall at the top of the beach in an attempt to hold back the Germans and enable as many of his men as possible to re-embark and make their way safely back to England.

It was because of his actions in repeatedly trying to inspire his men to cross the bridge by placing himself in clear sight of the German gunners, and his other acts of bravery at Dieppe, that Merritt was later awarded the Victoria Cross (see Chapter 10 for further details), even though his wartime combat had lasted for a total of just six hours.

Figures from the Saskatchewan Military Museum show that 81 men of the regiment were killed in action at Dieppe, 166 were wounded, and 87, which included Merritt and 8 of his fellow officers, were captured and taken prisoner. A further 174 survived and returned to England. In presenting these figures it is accepted that they may not be totally accurate, as similar records compiled by at least one other source vary slightly.

The War Diaries of the South Saskatchewan Regiment for the dates 18, 19, 20, and 23 August 1942, read as follows:

> 18 Aug 1942 – Warning order came through for Exercise Ford I.
> 19 Aug 1942 – At zero 0450 hours S. Sask. R. landed in France on raid.
> 20 Aug 1942 – First men reported back from raid on France at 0015 hrs. Muster parade at 1130 hrs. C.S.M Mathers; Cpl. McAllister, Lieut. J.S Edmondson, L/Cpl. Rutz, Pte. Fisher, Pte. Johnson. O.A. broadcasted to Canada on Dieppe Raid. Draft from 2 C.D.I.R.U. of 4 officers and 139 O.R.s.

23 Aug 1942 – Church parade at St. Mary's Church, Pullborough. Memorial Funeral Service at Brockwood for 2 Canadian Division soldiers who died from wounds sustained while on active operations in France.

Taking into account that this was the first time during the Second World War Canadian troops had seen action, the War Diaries of the South Saskatchewan Regiment are extremely brief. There is no mention of how many were killed, wounded, or captured, and the entry for 23 August concerning the funeral for the two soldiers who died of their wounds sustained during the raid, somewhat surprisingly does not even mention their names.

Meanwhile, the Queen's Own Cameron Highlanders, who had landed on Green Beach just after their comrades from the South Saskatchewan Regiment, had been tasked with capturing a small airfield at nearby St Austin to prevent the German defenders at Dieppe from being reinforced by air. They had also been tasked with taking out a German battery before joining up with other units and carrying out an attack on a German headquarters just south of Pourville. Although they managed to advance further inland than any other Allied unit throughout the course of the raid, they were, ironically, prevented from carrying out their tasks by German reinforcements who had been rushed to the area once they had realised an Allied raid was underway. This in itself had caused an element of uncertainty as to what exactly was going on as there was likely an initial concern that this was the beginning of a full-scale Allied invasion.

By the end of the raid, seventy-five members of the Camerons had been killed.

Orange Beach

The actions of No. 4 Commando and members of the 1st Battalion, US Army Rangers, under the command of the enigmatic Lord Lovat, was the one real success story of the raid on Dieppe. In essence, Lord Lovat and his men had been tasked with knocking out a German defensive battery situated at Blanc-Mesnil-Saint-Marguerite, near Varengeville, which they succeeded in doing. The complete details of No. 4 Commando's actions are covered in greater detail in Chapters 5 and 10.

CHAPTER FOUR

RAF Flight Sergeant Jack Nissenthall

One man who landed on Green Beach at Pourville with the South Saskatchewan Regiment was assigned a very important task. Flight Sergeant Jack Nissenthall was a radar specialist with the RAF, having worked in that particular field of electronics before the war.

Born on 9 October 1919 at Cottage Row, Bow, in the East End of London, Nissenthall's family roots were both Polish and Jewish. His father, Aaron Nissenthall, had emigrated to England from Poland in 1912, and in 1927 had applied to the Home Secretary to become a naturalised Englishman.

In 1936, when Jack was 17 years of age, he began an apprenticeship with the RAF. It was during this time that the respected radar expert, Robert Alexander Watson-Watt, who was later knighted by King George VI in 1942, was undertaking ground-breaking work on radio direction finding and radar technology; work that Nissenthall would have been involved to some degree.

At the outbreak of war in September 1939, Nissenthall, who was still only 18, like many men of his age wanted to do his bit for King and country. Having already served an apprenticeship with the RAF, this was the obvious service for him to join. He wanted excitement and so volunteered to serve as aircrew, but having already had his skills and worth in the field of electronics recognised, his request was denied. Instead, he found himself posted to RAF Yatesby, Wiltshire, which had been taken over by the Air Ministry at the outbreak of the war.

The base had three elements to it. Bomber aircraft wireless operators were trained there, the No. 2 Electrical and Wireless School RAF was housed there, as was radar training taught by No. 9 Radio School RAF. As for Nissenthall, he quickly became an important member of the base's Radio Direction Finding training wing, although between 1939 and the early part of 1942, he was posted to numerous different RAF bases around the country due to the acknowledgement by senior figures within the RAF of his wide spectrum of technical skills and abilities. It was whilst stationed at RAF Hope Grove, Devon, in 1942 that he played a leading role in the setting up of a Ground Control Intercept facility. This was part of the UK's air defence system and helped link radar and air observation stations to a central command centre so that incoming aircraft could be identified and attacked by RAF fighter squadrons, hopefully before they reached their intended target.

Nissenthall was certainly a determined character and despite his disappointment at having been refused the opportunity to undergo aircrew training, he still had aspirations to see active service on the battlefield and volunteered for Commando training just in case his particular skills were ever required to be used on enemy-held territory.

Sometime in the early part of 1942, Nissenthall was ordered to go to London to attend a meeting in Whitehall, where he would meet with members of the RAF Intelligence Section. Prior to leaving for London, he packed a small kit bag with a few belongings, including an avometer (an electrical measuring device), which had been given to him by his late father for his bar mitzvah. Sadly for Nissenthall, he would later lose the avometer during the raid.

One of those present at the meeting was Air Commodore Victor Tait, the RAF's Director of Signals and Radar. Mountbatten would have also been present, as was Ken Dearson, a member of his briefing team. At this meeting Nissenthall was under strict instructions not to reveal his name. The seriousness of what he was being asked to do and the potentially inherent dangers were fully explained to him, along with the fact that under no circumstances could they allow him to be captured alive because of the knowledge and information he possessed in relation to British and Allied radar capabilities. He was given the opportunity to think it over before returning the following day to give his answer.

On the morning of 5 July, after having given it due consideration, Nissenthall informed those who had interviewed him the previous day that he was happy to take part in the raid. He was then provided with an army revolver, an army khaki uniform, and a small tin which contained a number of items that it was felt might be of some use to him on the raid. This included a green suicide pill which he was expected to take in the event he was taken alive. After the meeting had been concluded, Nissenthall left in company with an unnamed member of the Special Executive Office (SOE), who drove him to Waterloo railway station, where he then caught a train to Southampton. On arrival he took a short bus journey to King George V dock area and caught a ferry to East Cowes on the Isle of Wight. On arrival, he was collected and taken to Norris Castle, where he met the Officer Commanding the South Saskatchewan Regiment, Lieutenant Colonel Charles Merritt. Despite Merritt's rank, and the fact he was in charge of the regiment, he was still not permitted to know Nissenthall's name. As well as being introduced to Merritt, Nissenthall also met the men, led by Sergeant Roy Hawkins, who had been detailed to act as his bodyguards for the duration of the mission. None of these men was told what his name was. The less anybody knew about him the better it was for all concerned. Nissenthall's bodyguard simply referred to him by the name of "Spook".

The following day, 6 July, Nissenthall, his personal bodyguard from A Company, and the rest of the South Saskatchewan men taking part in the raid, boarded the SS *Invicta* and the SS *Princess Beatrix* in preparation for what was believed to be training for the events of what were to come. It was only when the men were on board that they were informed they were on their way to France, where they would be disembarking the following morning. But before the excitement reached a fever pitch, the operation, then under the name of Rutter, was cancelled due to inclement weather. The anticipation at finally being able to have a go at the Germans was short lived and somewhat frustrating for those involved.

But all was not lost. Rather than being cancelled outright, the operation was renamed Jubilee and rescheduled to take place on 19 August. Once again Nissenthall was called down to London from his base in Devon, where he made his way to the headquarters of Combined Operations, situated at 1A Richmond Terrace. Once again, he was kitted out with what he would need for the raid, but this time instead of being driven to Waterloo railway station, he was taken straight to Southampton in the back of an officer's staff car, where the *Invicta* and the men of the South Saskatchewan Regiment were waiting for his arrival. It would not have been difficult for those on board, particularly the men of A Company tasked with looking after him, to have realised that with him there, this was not just another practice or an exercise, this was the real thing. It was happening at long last, their chance to engage their German counterparts and get some actual fighting under their belts. But after making their way across the English Channel and transferring into a landing craft some two hours from their intended target, the real drama had yet to begin.

The raid on Dieppe was a mission that 22-year-old Nissenthall happily volunteered for even though he knew the personal risks involved. For him there were only two options: to carry out his mission successfully and return to the beach, or be killed in action. Being taken prisoner was simply not an option. Because of his knowledge of British radar systems, he simply could not be allowed to be taken alive, which was one of the reasons he was provided with a cyanide capsule.

Along with the eleven men from A Company acting as his bodyguard, his job was to make his way to the radar station, get inside, and discover everything he could about the radar system that the Germans were using.

What is clear is that Nissenthall's bodyguards had all been told that if it looked like he was about to be captured, or was wounded and could not be moved, they were to kill him. However, the main aspect of their role was obviously to help get him to the radar installation safely so that he could carry out his task. As there was no guarantee that any or all of the Saskatchewan soldiers would survive the mission themselves, it made sense to give the order to kill Nissenthall to all his bodyguards, rather than to just one man.

Nissenthall's mission was certainly never going to be easy. He and his group first had to make it safely to the beach in their landing craft, praying that they were not struck by German artillery shells as they did so. This was a real possibility because the German 'Freya' radar station at Pourville could cover a distance of up to 125 miles, meaning that the likelihood of the landing craft not being seen by the radar operators as they approached Dieppe was extremely unlikely.

Besides the men of A Company, three other companies of the 1st Battalion, South Saskatchewan Regiment were involved in the raid. The job of C Company was to take and hold the village of Pourville, whilst B and D companies had been tasked with putting in place a perimeter defensive line further inland in an effort to prevent German reinforcements from reaching the centre of the village.

As soon as the landing craft dropped their ramps, the German defenders opened up with their MG34 belt-fed machine guns, which fired a staggering 900 rounds per minute. This was the welcome the men of the South Saskatchewan received as they disembarked. For a number of them, their war was over even before they had set foot on the beach. Wounded and dead were quickly strewn across the entrance of the landing craft, on the beach, and in the water. But despite the panic, fear and confusion that would have momentarily enveloped those who were still alive, they needed to quickly regain their composure and make it up the beach to the relative safety of the seawall as fast as they could if they wanted to stay alive.

The first thing that would have been clear to the officers, if not the men as well, was they had not landed at their intended destination: the foot of the Freya cliff. Instead, the Royal Navy landing craft had dropped them right in the middle of the heavily defended village of Pourville, making their mission even more dangerous than it was intended to be. Because of the predicament they found themselves in, there was now no guarantee they would even make it off the beach, let alone continue on to achieve their objective.

For those who made it to the seawall, there was at least the opportunity to catch their breath and quickly work out what they were now going to do and which direction they had to head to achieve their individual tasks.

Nissenthall and his bodyguards now had to make their way through the village, up to the radar station on the cliffs above the town, whilst all the time hoping they would avoid being hit and killed by the continuous threat of German mortar, machine gun and sniper fire. Then and only then, did Nissenthall even have a chance of completing his mission. Add to this the fact that this was the first time he or any of his bodyguards had ever seen real, live, action, the chances of any of them actually surviving the mission were slim at best.

If the landing craft bringing the men of the Saskatchewan Regiment ashore had done so at the right location, not only would the raid have gone more according to plan than it did, but the regiment would have sustained fewer casualties by the time the raid was over.

Nissenthall's first challenge was to climb up the seawall, cross over the road, and for him and the men of A Company to make their way as quickly as they could to the radar station. Thankfully, when they reached the top of the seawall, they only found themselves confronted with a reel of barbed wire rather than the sound of withering machine gun fire from the buildings on the other side of the road.

Nissenthall and his minders were to the rear of the Saskatchewans as they set off into the village and beyond via a bridge that was heavily defended. It was here that a number of Canadian soldiers were killed and wounded as the bottleneck of the bridge hampered their progress, thus making them easy targets for the German defenders. It was here that Lieutenant Colonel Merritt's actions led to him being awarded the Victoria Cross for putting himself in plain sight of the Germans so as to rally his men and get them across the bridge and beyond. There was a quiet eeriness and a growing feeling of anticipation about the situation, but neither feeling lasted for very long as machine gun fire from an enemy pillbox left a number of the Canadians dead, dying and wounded in the street. Suddenly, a break in the firing led to one of the Canadians, without any order to do so, to break cover, rush forward and accurately place a grenade through the firing slit of the pillbox. The subsequent explosion took care of those inside.

With the pillbox now nothing more than a large piece of reinforced, smoke-filled concrete, the remaining members of the Saskatchewan Regiment continued their mission, but by then a number of Nissenthall's bodyguards had already been killed or wounded.

To reach the top of the cliff they had to make their way up and along a grassy track. By now there was very little in the way of cover other than that provided by the smoke grenades they threw ahead of them. The closer the South Saskatchewans got to the cliff top, the fewer of them were left to continue the fight. Only seven of the men guarding Nissenthall were still fit enough to continue, whilst the rest of A Company had not fared much better: out of the 100 who had arrived at Dieppe, only 25 of them had not been killed or wounded, whilst all the time machine gun fire and mortar shells continuously rained down upon them.

As the South Saskatchewans finally made it to the top of the cliff, immediately ahead of them was the heavily guarded Freya radar station. Getting across the open ground, through or over the reels of protective barbed wire would be difficult enough, while avoiding the raking bursts of machine gun fire from the German defenders, who had the added protection of being behind a combination of sandbags and trenches, was not going to make things any easier.

The reality was that by the time Nissenthall reached the top of the cliff and had the radar station in plain sight, the fight put up by the German defenders meant that many of the men detailed to protect him were either dead or wounded, and with only a small number of other South Saskatchewans still with them, there was no possibility of being able to carry out any kind of effective raid on the installation.

Nissenthall was able to tell the radar's capabilities simply by looking at it, but that information did not make the situation any less complicated than it already was. It was imperative that he got closer to it, or inside if possible, to be able to fully understand its finite capabilities. But he had a dilemma as there were so few men of A Company left to accompany him who had not been killed or wounded.

It would have been both easier and completely understandable for Jack Nissenthall to have quit there and then, and for him to have made his way back down to the beach to await to be evacuated to England. Instead, he and two of his minders decided to make their way back to the centre of Pourville, despite knowing full well that to attempt to do so would make them immediate targets for any German soldiers in the area. But it was something that had to be done if the mission had any chance of being successful. If they could reach their headquarters situated in the casino, close to the beach, then they could at the very least arrange for a naval bombardment of the area immediately surrounding the radar station. Unfortunately for Nissenthall and his comrades, however, it was not possible to make radio contact with any of the Royal Navy vessels off the coast of Dieppe.

Despite eventually being able to return to the top of the cliff with a mortar team, where Captain Murray Osten and the remaining men of A Company were waiting, it was not possible to get close enough to the radar station for them to be effective because of the strength and fire-power of its defences.

Nissenthall knew that even if the radar station could not be captured for him to get inside to have a look at its inner most secrets, and to physically take evidence of the important parts of the radar away, his mission could still prove to be worthwhile. He knew that if he could get close enough to it, then his efforts might just prove extremely beneficial to the Allied war effort, but it would be dangerous and possibly cost him his life.

But this did not deter him. Armed with only a service revolver, a couple of grenades and a few tools, he left the relative safety of his position and, by crawling on his hands and knees, with his body as close to the ground as he could possibly get, he slowly made his way round to the rear of the radar station. Despite German machine gun positions trying their best to kill him, he eventually managed to get to within 50 yards of the building, locate the exposed telephone lines, and cut them through. This meant that the only way those inside the radar station could communicate with nearby commanders was by way of radio. This was good news for the Allies, because any subsequent transmissions that were then sent by the Germans were immediately intercepted, overheard and translated by the numerous RAF listening posts spread out across the south coast of England.

Having achieved his goal, Nissenthall crawled back round to the front of the radar station to discover that nearly all the members of A Company had either been wounded or killed, and that nearly all of the remaining uninjured were the members of his escort detail. But Nissenthall was not finished: he still wanted to try to get inside the German radar station. He then had the idea of once again making his way back in to Pourville, but this time to find and commandeer a tank so that he could once again return to the radar site to try to blast a hole through its outer wall. What he did not know, of course, was that none of the Canadian tanks had actually made it that far off the beach before either braking down or being put out of action.

What the commanding officer of A Company thought of Nissenthall's madcap idea is not recorded, but he certainly did not take any chances once he agreed to let him go. To ensure his safety, or to make sure that he did not fall into the hands of the Germans, he sent all seven of his surviving minders along with him. After reaching the nearby village of Petit-Appeville, which was still 2 miles from Pourville, Nissenthall and his guards suddenly heard the sound of tanks coming their way, thankful at the belief that the landed Churchill tanks had made it off of the beach and were pushing inland. The problem was that when the tanks came in to view, they were German Panzers.

The initial euphoria felt by Nissenthall and his escort upon hearing the advancing tanks was quickly replaced with fear and trepidation when they suddenly saw what they were up against. In the ensuing fire fight, two of Nissenthall's escort were shot and killed. Meanwhile, he experienced a miraculous piece of good fortune when he was struck by a bullet on the back of his steel helmet, but suffered nothing more than a glancing blow, with the bullet ricocheting away, leaving him lucky to still be alive.

Without too much time to spare, Nissenthall and his minders quickly made their escape, but not before they had been seen by the enemy. They ran off in the direction of Pourville as quickly as their legs would carry them, with bullets whizzing past as they ran. By the time they reached their destination, three more of his minders had fallen, but in the circumstances, there was no time to stop to check on each fallen man's condition.

From this point in time Nissenthall knew there was no point in trying to return to the Freya radar station to try to illicit any more useful intelligence from it. If he wanted to stay alive, he had to make his way back to the beach as quickly as possible to have any chance of being evacuated. He certainly had no desire to find out whether or not his minders were actually prepared to shoot him.

The difficulty for the Canadians at this time was that they had to split their forces between those fighting a rear guard action whilst at the same time keeping a solid enough perimeter far enough away from the beaches at Pourville. Not to mention the challenge of getting as many of their wounded and abled bodied men back on board their landing craft and evacuate them back across the English Channel to safety. If Nissenthall wanted to stay alive, he had to ensure that he was one of them.

The casino which earlier in the raid had been the Canadians' headquarters now became a much-needed casualty clearing station to deal with the ever-increasing number of Canadian wounded. The dilemma for the retreating Canadians was how long did they keep up their defensive positions before making a run for the beach? Both the Navy and RAF were doing their bit to try to keep the German forces pinned down so as to facilitate the escape of what remained of the raiding party. The trick was when to pick their moment to make their escape. At least one landing craft remained some way offshore, and dare not come in any closer for fear of being attacked.

It was now late morning and the time had come to stop talking and make a decision. But as luck would have it, and with timing being as perfect as it could have possibly been, a smoke shell fired from the Royal Navy destroyer HMS *Brocklesby* exploded on the beach, providing the immediate and necessary cover required. Nissenthall and his colleagues, including Sergeant Roy Hawkins, did not need any further encouragement and decided that it was time to make a dash for it.

This final part of the journey was the most dangerous. Their race for freedom began from the safety of the casino, before running as fast as they could towards the seawall, across the stony beach to the shore line and on towards the landing craft, knowing full well that once in the open they were vulnerable to the German machine gun positions high up on the cliffs. To try to assist in this process, HMS *Brocklesby* opened up with her 4-inch guns. The accuracy of her shooting had the desired effect with a round hitting its intended target, causing part of the cliff to disintegrate. The German positions that were still intact quickly realised that to have any chance of not suffering the same fate, they had to stop firing so that their positions would not be identified.

The outer perimeter defences around Pourville were gradually overcome by the advancing German forces. In doing so, the closer they subsequently got to the harbour and beach area meant the more accurate and concentrated their gunfire was. By the time Nissenthall made it onto the beach, he was accompanied by just one of his minders, Sergeant Hawkins. They were now the only members of A Company to have taken part in the raid who had not been killed or captured. The landing craft they were running towards had already started to reverse off the beach, but there was no turning back now.

The time it took Nissenthall to cross the beach was quite possibly the most important few seconds of his life. Despite being with one of his minders and having a cyanide capsule to ensure that he was never taken alive, he also had the two hand grenades he had taken with him when he went to cut the wires at the radar station attached to his side, intending to detonate them if he were wounded or captured as he made his way to the landing craft.

On reaching the water's edge, both Nissenthall and Hawkins dived full length into the water and kept swimming until they reached the landing craft, where they were eventually hauled on board by a couple of young, brave and willing sailors. The beach was still covered in a cloud of smoke, affording the landing craft and those on board some protection as they made their way out to sea, but it did not prevent German aircraft from being able to attack them.

Nissenthall's badly damaged landing craft eventually made it to the *Brocklesby*, and although the Luftwaffe still continued their attacks, the vessel made it safely back to Newhaven late the following day.

Not all the Canadians made it to the safety of the landing crafts. Some remained behind in Pourville to continue the rear-guard action in an effort to try to keep the Germans at bay. This was only sustainable for so long, but the longer they managed to keep the advancing Germans at bay, the more of their comrades would manage to escape. By 13.00, the remaining Canadian forces had run out of ammunition and had no other option but to lay down their arms and surrender. The most senior man of those left behind was Lieutenant Colonel Merritt. After surrendering, the Canadians were lined up in the street in front of the Hotel de la Terrasse, before being marched off into captivity. The majority of the men would spend the rest of the war as prisoners.

Once on board the landing craft, Nissenthall and the rest of the Canadians who had managed to escape the beach were still not safe. Doing their best to prevent the Canadians from escaping, the Luftwaffe continually attacked and strafed the landing craft, causing so much damage that soon after the men were transferred to a waiting destroyer further out to sea, it fell beneath the waves and sank.

It was 02.00 in the early hours of 20 August when the ship Jack Nissenthall was on finally arrived at Newhaven. What was left of the night saw Nissenthall and his one remaining bodyguard, Sergeant Hawkins, find somewhere to get their heads down for a well-earned sleep, both happy in the knowledge that Nissenthall was now no longer under the threat of death.

But Nissenthall's problems were not quite at an end. The anonymity of his task and the importance of remaining nameless initially worked against him. All the returning Canadian soldiers were individually debriefed on their return at the Canadian Army headquarters in Reigate, Surrey. Despite Nissenthall being English and not Canadian, he also found himself having to face questioning, but unable to confirm his identity, and dressed in a combination of different items of uniform, including a Royal Marine jacket, regulation British

Army trousers and an RAF shirt, he initially raised a few eyebrows amongst the Canadian military intelligence officers tasked with conducting his debrief. Eventually, however, he was able to persuade them that he was not a German POW attempting to conceal his true identity.

On the morning of 20 August, having grabbed a few hours' sleep but still dishevelled and unshaven from his exploits at Dieppe, Nissenthall caught a train to London's Waterloo station before making his way on the Underground to the Air Ministry, located at Adastral House, at the junction of Kingsway and Aldwych. There he underwent a full debrief about his actions at Dieppe. Two of the people who were waiting for him were Air Commodore Victor Hubert Tait, who was also the Director-General of Signals, which incorporated Radio Direction Finding, and Professor Reginald V. Jones, a British radar expert and a member of the RAF's intelligence section.

The single most important invention which came about as a direct result of Nissenthall's actions at Dieppe was Allied electronic jamming equipment, which provided the Allies with a massive aerial advantage that was fully utilised during the Normandy landings of June 1944. In cutting the radar station landline communication cables, Nissenthall forced the Germans inside to send their messages by radio, which were then intercepted back in England. Subsequent German radio transmissions were also intercepted by the British, which provided valuable intelligence and information about German radar systems, thus allowing the British to design and develop electronic jamming equipment.

Nissenthall served in the RAF throughout the rest of the war and even set up a defensive radar system for Allied forces in the Middle East. But he was never again called upon to utilise his Commando training and deploy on any similar raids. At the time of the raid, Nissenthall possibly knew more detailed and sensitive information about Allied radar systems than any man alive. Allowing himself to be captured by the Germans was simply not an outcome that could be allowed to happen. Nissenthall knew this before he set out on the mission, showing genuine bravery and heroism in the face of adversity, especially for someone so young.

Meanwhile, Captain Osten, the man in charge of A Company during the raid on Dieppe, was one of those taken prisoner. He spent the rest of the war in captivity before being liberated on 12 April 1945. Some years after the war the two men met up. Osten told Nissenthall that when he had first been informed that under no circumstances was he to allow him to be taken alive, he was surprised and shocked. After all, just how valuable and important could an RAF sergeant possibly be to the Allied war effort? Nissenthall then asked Osten whether he would have followed orders and shot him to avoid him being taken prisoner. 'Yes', Osten replied, 'I probably would.'

CHAPTER FIVE

1st Battalion, US Army Rangers at Dieppe

The 1st Ranger Battalion was officially brought into being on 19 June 1942 and its first commander was Captain William Orlando Darby, a graduate from West Point in 1933, who was given just a few weeks to get the unit organised.

The new force trained at the British Commando Training Centre at Achnacarry in Scotland, which made perfect sense as it was on the British Commandos that the US Rangers were styled. Approximately 2,000 American soldiers volunteered, but few met the exacting standards expected of those needed to serve in the Rangers.

For those 600 men who had what it took, they next had to be put through their paces by the more experienced British Commandos. This involved a strict medical examination and intensive and physically demanding training, which included long marches in difficult conditions. The training was overseen by British Army Colonel Charles Vaughan MBE, with all of his instructors being battle-hardened British Commandos. By the end of the process, 500 men had proved themselves enough to have passed the course, which had certainly not been for the feint hearted. One man was killed and several others wounded after the training was carried out using live ammunition. The Rangers had, quite literally, received a baptism of fire, and a type of training American soldiers had never previously experienced. These men would now become the 1st Ranger Battalion and were nicknamed Darby's Rangers, after their commander.

The battalion was divided in to six companies:

A (Able) Company
B (Bravo) Company
C (Charlie) Company
D (Dog) Company
E (Easy) Company
F (Fox) Company

Fifty officers and enlisted men of the Rangers were chosen for the ill-fated raid on Dieppe, making them the first United States soldiers to fight against the Germans on the ground anywhere in the European theatre. Three of the group were killed, a further three were captured, and five were wounded.

The inclusion of American forces in the raid on Dieppe was not part of the original planning for the operation. The 1st Ranger Battalion had only been formed in June 1942, with the original idea being for them to be no more than a temporary unit who would gain combat experience and disseminate what they had learned, good or bad, and pass it on to new American fighting units. With the United States becoming more involved in the war, the Rangers were added to the operation so that they could gain this much-needed combat experience.

The title of "Ranger" was selected by American Army officer Lieutenant General Lucian K. Truscott, who, when giving his reason for choosing it, said the following:

> I selected "Rangers" because few words have a more glamorous connotation in American Military history. It was therefore fitting that the organisation destined to be the first of the American ground forces to battle Germans on the European Continent in World War II should be called Rangers, in compliment to those in American history who exemplified such high standards of individual courage, initiative, determination and ruggedness, fighting ability, and achievement.

Captain Darby, the man initially selected to take command of the newly formed 1st Ranger Battalion, was an ideal candidate. He was recognised by his senior officers to be both intelligent and enthusiastic. He was an artillery officer who had operational experience with both cavalry and infantry units, as well as having also undergone amphibious training. Knowing the exact type of individuals he wanted for his new unit, Darby took part in the interviewing of those officers and men who had put themselves forward to be Rangers. The main elements he was looking for in those he selected was an athletic build, and to be physically in good condition. Age was not an issue for him, as was proven in those he selected, whose ages ranged from 17 to 35. He was not just looking for infantry soldiers either. Besides the 34th Infantry Division, others were selected from the 1st Armored Division, as well as anti-aircraft units.

A number of the Americans who took part in the raid on Dieppe displayed exemplary courage and bravery, some of whom received official recognition for their actions. The Rangers themselves did not operate as an independent unit, but instead were split up amongst some of the other units. The main purpose for their inclusion was for them to gain valuable first-hand combat experience so that they could, in turn, help train other Rangers based on their own experiences gained at Dieppe. Forty of the Rangers were attached to No. 3 Commando, who had a particulary difficult time. Although thirty-five of the Rangers did not even make it to the beaches, fifteen of them did. Along with their British colleagues they made it to the top of the cliffs, only to find themselves up against a much larger enemy, which forced them to retreat back to the beach. Other Rangers were attached to No. 4 Commando, who overall had a more successful day. Of the Rangers who made it to shore, three were killed, another three were captured, whilst a further five were wounded.

CHAPTER SIX

French Civilians and the Dieppe Raid

One of the aspects about the raid on Dieppe which is rarely mentioned is the price paid by the civilian population. By the time of the raid, areas of northern France and its people had been under German occupation for more than two years, a period of time which had been far from pleasant. Earlier in 1942, a number of the town's residents had already lost their homes and businesses when the Germans demolished part of the seafront buildings to aid in their coastal defence system. Then, less than three weeks after the raid, on 11 September 1942, a mass round up of hundreds of individuals by the German authorities led to many civilians being taken to Mechelen, Belgium, which was a large transit camp for prisoners who were waiting to be transported to the death camps in Poland.

In the planning for the original raid, Operation Rutter, one of the plan's elements had been an aerial bombardment of the town of Dieppe. After the plans had been re-jigged, due in part to prolonged inclement weather and Mountbatten's insistence on it still going ahead, despite the reluctance of Montgomery and the Chiefs of Staff, it became known as Operation Jubilee. One of the major changes was to take out the proposed bombing raid on the town before the amphibious forces landed due to major concerns about the large numbers of French civilians that were likely to be killed and how that would potentially change the relationship between the Allies and the French civilian population. Despite this change to the plan, the RAF and USAAF still lost six of its bomber aircraft, along with a total of ninety-four of its fighter aircraft.

How much information, if any, the local population knew about the raid beforehand is unclear, but it is unlikely they would have been pre-warned of any such attack. They may have had an inkling of potential Allied interest in the town because of the large numbers of German troops stationed there, more than 1,500 in total, and the number of defensive positions which covered the port area and the adjacent beaches that were constantly manned by the Germans.

Despite a radio transmission on the BBC announcing an imminent raid was due to take place somewhere along the west coast of France, for security reasons it was not possible to inform the population of Dieppe that it was their town where the raid would take place, and when. The other concern was how they would react to the actual raid once they saw Allied soldiers fighting their way through the town. The worry was that once these troops had been seen, coupled with the incoming artillery shells and aircraft in the skies above, the town's residents would misinterpret what was going on and think it was a full-scale invasion of France. Civilians seen to be actively helping Allied soldiers during the raid, having mistaken it for an invasion, would have been dealt with severely by German forces in the immediate aftermath of the raid, with potentially dire consequences for the entire population.

The first time the local population would have been aware that something was happening would have been in the early hours of 19 August 1942, as the first Allied aircraft began attacking German coastal artillery at 04.16, when the darkness of the night made the bombing accuracy of the attacking aircraft hard to confirm. This was followed shortly afterwards by the dropping of a number of smoke bombs around the German gun batteries on the cliff areas on the eastern side of the town. The effectiveness of the smoke screen was assisted by crops which had been set on fire as a result of the Allied attack. The confusion for the civilian population would have no doubt been added to by the somewhat deafening sound of the German anti-aircraft guns, which had quickly burst into action to try to shoot down the attacking Allied aircraft.

In the immediate aftermath of the fighting, large numbers of French civilians were allowed by the Germans to recover the dead bodies of Allied soldiers and prepare them for burial, sparing them the grim task of having to do it themselves.

One person who was particularly happy that the local population had not joined in the fighting on the Allied side was none other than Adolf Hitler. He was so happy, in fact, that he decided to release some 750 French POWs originally from Dieppe and allow them to return to their homes and families. He also provided financial assistance in the form of 10 million French francs to help pay for the damage which had been caused to homes and properties in the town, as a direct result of the raid.

It was not unusual for civilians to become casualties of war, and the raid on Dieppe was no different. Forty-eight of the town's civilian population were killed during the raid. The complete list of names of those who were killed are recorded in Appendix G at the back of this book. However, details of a few of those who were killed are recorded below, with extracts taken from David Raillot's book *Greges: Yesterday, today, or the history of a Village in Upper Normandy*, which includes the operation report of Dr Poupault and the testimony of Madame Burette's grand-daughter, Madame Claude Auvray-Hedoux.

> Two fighter aircraft were chasing each other in the skies over Greges. One of the two bombs fell on a barn on Madeleine Burette's farm; the other landed in the kitchen of the farm house. The splinters pierced the floor of the room located on the first floor, in which were Mrs Burette (52) and her 22-year-old daughter, Jeanine. The daughter was transported to the clinic of Dr Poupault before being transferred to the hospital at Lintot-Les-Bois, where the injuries to her right arm were treated and she survived.
>
> As for Mrs Burette, despite her medical treatment, she suffered an acute anemia. She was wounded in the abdomen but died from an internal haemorrhage.

Fernand Gode, 31, was busy mowing oats in a field in the village of Sauchay-Le-Haut when a German aircraft machine gunned him and his horses. The horses were only wounded, but Monsieur Gode was killed.

The following is taken from the memoirs of M. Marie-Jeanne Leblond, which were included in the book by Franco Gueho, *One Hundred Years in Berneval*.

> We heard screams and cries for help. It was Monsieur and Madam Joseph Grout who had returned to their home after a night spent at Monsieur Bimont's farm. An incendiary bomb fell on the luggage rack

of Monsieur Grout's bike, which was surrounded by flames, and his wife struggled to get him off the bike. Monsieur Grout was horribly burnt; we brought him back to the charcuterie. I knew that presumably he had received a phosphorus bomb as he had flames all over his body.

Clemence Meunier's home was in a street near the Place Duparchy overlooking the beach. Having heard a lot of noise outside she suddenly opened her window shutters in the room making them slam against the wall. Nearby, thinking he had heard a gunshot, a German soldier opened fire in her direction, killing her instantly.

In the years that followed the war, when Canadian veterans who survived the raid re-visited Dieppe on the anniversary of that fateful day, thousands of local residents lined the streets to show their respect for both those who had survived and the 916 Canadian soldiers who were killed. There are several memorials, including a park situated on the promenade in the centre the town, to ensure the price paid and sacrifice made by hundreds of brave young men is never forgotten.

A memorial to the memory of the Canadian Soldiers was unveiled in Dieppe on 23 August 2015, which included the following testimony.

Operation Jubilee

During the raid of August 19, 1942, 46 civilians perished among the population of region, 13 were under the age of twenty. *Don't forget them...*

CHAPTER SEVEN

German Defenders at Dieppe

An important aspect of the Second World War was intelligence, but keeping things completely secret was not always possible, especially when it came to anything undertaken on a large scale. From a combination of aerial reconnaissance photographs, and no doubt one or two of their spies operating along the south coast of England, the Germans became aware of a concentration of naval landing craft being assembled at a number of southern ports.

Radio messages had been transmitted by the BBC informing the French people of an imminent raid somewhere along the west coast of France, but it did not specify where it would take place or when. The reason for this transmission was to emphasise to the French people that this was purely a raid and not a full-scale invasion.

Armed with such information, German forces deployed in French coastal regions, including such places as the Pas de Calais, Cherbourg, St Malo, and Le Havre, were on high alert, with defensive positions being manned 24 hours a day throughout the summer of 1942.

On the day of the raid leaflets were distributed amongst the town's civilian population, once again pointing out that the action that day was simply a raid and nothing more, and that under no circumstances should they become involved.

There would have been an expectation by the raiding force that they would be met by some kind of German resistance, but because of poor intelligence reports, the strength of what they would be up against had been severely underestimated. The other unknown element of the raid was how quickly the Germans would respond to the raid, which to an extent would be driven by the level of surprise.

Probably unbeknown to the Allied raiding party, waiting to greet them on the beaches at Dieppe were somewhere in the region of 2,000 men of the 302nd Static Infantry Division, made up of men from Military District No. II, in the Stettin area of north-east Germany.

The division had been formed in November 1940 and the German military authorities had decided to use them as a French occupying unit. When they arrived in France, they were allocated to a sector some 70 kilometres wide in the area around Dieppe. The man in charge of the division was Generalleutnant Konrad Haase, who took command on 15 November 1940 and remained with them until 26 November 1942. Before the war he had held the rank of Oberstleutnant in the Dresden Police.

The division was made up of elements from the following units:

570th Infantry Regiment
571st Infantry Regiment
572nd Infantry Regiment
302nd Reconnaissance Battalion

302nd Anti-tank Battalion
302nd Artillery Regiment
302nd Engineer Regiment
302nd Signal Battalion
265th Heavy Infantry Howitzer Battery
813th Army Coastal Battery (Varengeville)

Half the men were set up to defend the harbour and beach area, as well as the town, whilst the others were placed further inland and on higher ground where they manned a number of designated defensive positions consisting of machine gun nests and heavy artillery batteries. The area they covered was about 16 kilometers in width, either side of Dieppe.

The latter of these units, the 813th Army Coastal Battery at Varengeville, were attacked from all sides by Lord Lovat, Major Derek Mills-Roberts, and the 252 men of No. 4 Commando with mortars, machine guns, sub-machine guns, and hand-grenades. They were supported in their task by low-flying RAF air attacks, with the combination of a ground and air attack helping to keep the battery in check. During this sustained attack the battery's artillery shells, which were stored in the ammunition pit, were set on fire. Despite this, the Germans defended their position gallantly, resulting in fifty-seven casualties, including twenty-eight killed. A testimony to the heroic defence of their position.

The Germans had set up heavy machine gun positions on the pier and in several seafront properties, from where they could cover a wide area either side of the harbour entrance. This would have made the task of the Allied soldiers coming ashore in that area, mainly the Canadians, very dangerous and extremely difficult. Many would be lucky to make it across the beach and to the relative safety of the beach wall. Raising their heads, even just to get a glimpse of the direction they were going, would potentially have had fatal consequences.

The Germans also had the following units in reserve to use as the need required:

    676th Infantry Regiment (Headquarters Section) – Doudeville
    676th Infantry Regiment, 1st Battalion – Hericourt
    676th Infantry Regiment, 3rd Battalion – Yvetot
    570th Infantry Regiment, 3rd Battalion – Bacqueville
    81st Tank Company – Yvetot
    1st (Artillery) Battalion, 332nd Infantry Division.

The raid began at 05.00, and the waters of the English Channel had been relatively calm as the vessels made their way to Dieppe. When they were a few hundred yards from the shore, Canadian and British soldiers climbed down the side of the Royal Navy destroyers they had been on board into the smaller, lighter landing craft, which then landed them on the beaches whilst it was still dark.

Regardless of what the British and Canadians were expecting, the Germans defended resiliently and in just over nine hours, had forced their attackers to retreat back into the sea. Those who had not escaped had either been killed or captured. The number of German casualties, both killed and wounded, was somewhere in the region of 600 men.

In the immediate aftermath of the raid, an unknown German army major went down to the beach at Dieppe, accompanied by a number of his colleagues, to inspect the resultant carnage and no doubt express a semblance of professional disbelief at what had taken place. What the major and his colleagues saw was not pleasant, even for experienced soldiers:

I have not witnessed images more terrible. In one landing craft the entire crew of about forty men had been wiped out by a direct hit. On the water we could see bits of wrecks, ships in ruin, corpses floating and soldiers wrestling with death. In Paris there was jubilation. The enemy's operation was smashed in just over nine hours.

After their successful defence of Dieppe, the 302nd Infantry Division acquired a commanding reputation amongst their colleagues from other units. Rather aptly, they became known as the 'Dieppe Division', a nickname they were proud to bare.

The division's success came at a price, and not one they would have necessarily wanted to pay. In January 1943, the entire division, which by then had increased in size, was moved from the relative tranquillity of western France and sent to the Eastern Front as part of the Kharkov Offensive. The division remained on the Eastern Front as Soviet forces eventually gained the upper hand, forcing the German forces to retreat back to the River Dnieper. It was whilst attempting to retreat further west on 25 August 1944 that the division was surrounded by Soviet forces and its men were either captured or killed.

As part of their duties, the German defenders at Dieppe were tasked with manning a total of five batteries, which had all been designed and built with the expectation of dealing with a threat from the sea. The batteries were at different locations in and around the Dieppe area and were simply known to the Germans by the name of the town or village where they were situated. The Allies, on the other hand, had selected nicknames for each of the batteries.

The battery at Berneval had been given the name of Goebbels by the Allied planners, after the Nazi minister for propaganda, Joseph Goebbels. It was a massive site, equipped with three 170-mm guns, four 105-mm guns, as well as a number of 20-mm Flak guns, which provided a powerful and impressive defensive platform. If left intact, the battery's potential destructive power was almost unthinkable. Indeed, this one battery alone was so big it required around 250 men to operate it to its full capacity.

The Puys Battery had been named Rommel, after the respected German General, Erwin Rommel. This was equipped with four 155-mm guns as well as three 88-mm guns.

The Calnon Battery, which consisted of four 150-mm guns and three 88-mm guns, had been nicknamed Hitler.

The Ferme des 4 Vents (Janval) Battery had been nicknamed Hindenburg, after Paul von Hindenburg, the former German Army officer and German President, and was armed with a number of 75-mm guns.

The Varengeville Battery had the nickname of Hess, after Rudolph Hess, the Deputy Führer of Nazi Germany between 1933 and 1941. The battery here consisted of six 155-mm guns as well as seven 20-mm Flak guns.

German documents which were subsequently recovered proved that German forces at Dieppe had no prior knowledge of the raid taking place, even though they must have known that some kind of action might occur due to the increase in shipping traffic and the intercepted radio messages. The first the Germans had any idea that an attack was imminent was when some of the British naval vessels making their way across the English Channel came into contact with a German convoy at 04.00 on the morning of the raid. There is no evidence to suggest that any of the convoy vessels messaged their colleagues inland to make them aware of what was happening. From captured German prisoners who were brought back to England, intelligence was obtained that the alarm at Dieppe was not sounded until nearly an hour after the convoy encounter.

One of the advantages the Germans had at Dieppe was that as well as the presence of three infantry battalions, the 81st Tank Company was stationed at Yvetot, a French commune in the Normandy region, halfway between Dieppe and Le Havre. The Allies had absolutely no knowledge that there was a German tank company anywhere near Dieppe.

During the raid, the Germans undertook several counterattacks against the raiding Allies forces. For some reason, however, they chose not to carry out any counterattack against Lovat's No. 4 Commando at Varengeville, whose attack on the battery at that location was the most successful part of the raid. The lack of a counterattack by the Germans in this instance could have been because they felt that heavily armed and well-protected artillery batteries were more than capable of looking after themselves, or that by the time they had realised the battery at Varengeville was under attack, the raiding party had already left and was on its way back to the beach.

Elements of the 571st German Infantry followed the retreat of the Queen's Own Cameron Highlanders towards Pourville, and later compiled a report criticising the Camerons for their slowness. The German report suggested that a more 'prompt and determined' attack towards Pourville by the Camerons would have produced a much better outcome for them.

German reports confirm that No. 5 and No. 11 companies of the 571st Infantry Regiment, along with elements of the 2nd Pioneer Company of the 302nd Division, carried out a counterattack against British forces as they attempted to escape via landing craft on the beaches. Once it was clear to the Germans that all the Allied troops who had taken part in the raid had been killed, captured or had escaped, they continued to remain in their defensive positions. Large numbers of German troops from both the 302nd Infantry Division and the reserve from the 676th Infantry Regiment remained in the areas of Pourville and St Aubin as a precaution, 'because of the many messages on hand reporting strong formations of ships en route from England', possibly in the belief that the Allied raid was merely the start of what could be a full-scale invasion. Why the Germans should have believed that such an event was likely to take place is unclear, taking into account that by this time they already possessed a copy of the Operational Order, which clearly would have made absolutely no mention of a second attack.

The report came to be in German hands after Canadian Brigadier William Wallace Southam, the commanding officer of the 6th Canadian Infantry Brigade, 2nd Canadian Division, brought a copy of the assault plan ashore with him, despite it being classified as a secret document. Immediately prior to surrendering, Southam tried to bury it under the pebbles on the beach, but was spotted by an eagle-eyed German soldier, who quickly retrieved it and handed it to his superiors. Somewhat remarkably, instead of being rebuked or criticised for this action, Southam was awarded the Distinguished Service Order (DSO) for his role in the operation, but would remain a POW for the rest of the war.

The Germans were far from impressed with the content of the Allied Operational Order, believing it was far too detailed and thus somewhat difficult to visualise. German intelligence reports remarked, 'the planning down to the last detail limits the independence of action of the subordinate officers and leaves them no opportunity to make independent decisions in an altered situation'. This is quite a sweeping statement to make as in numerous such events during the Second World War, original plans quite often never went according to plan, and so officers and men had to think on their feet and adapt quickly to the situations they found themselves in.

The Germans were very surprised to discover that the Allies had chosen not to use paratroopers as part of their attack, although this element had been included in the original plan for Operation Rutter, but had subsequently been removed because of concerns over the weather conditions at the time of the raid. They were also extremely surprised at the Allied decision to land the main body of the attacking force, including tanks, in the centre of Dieppe, especially as the strength of the German defences at that location were known prior to the raid taking place. They also felt that 'a few assault guns would probably have been more use to the British in their first attack than the tanks'.

The Germans noted that they felt it was a mistake that the Allied forces who landed near Pourville were not supported by tanks. They also commented at some length about the failure of the Camerons to push on to the St Aubin airfield, which they believed was because their commander, Major Laws, had become aware that the attacks at Puys and Dieppe had failed. In making their comments, the Germans did not mention the strength of their own defensive artillery units that the Camerons had found themselves up against.

The German conclusion about the Allied raid at Dieppe was as follows: 'The operation failed, primarily because in PUITS [Puys] the landing was repulsed, in DIEPPE the tanks did not succeed in crossing the anti-tank wall, and near POURVILLE the British battalions did not continue their advance.'

CHAPTER EIGHT

The RAF and the Dieppe Raid

During the raid on Dieppe, air support played an important part as it included fighters, bombers and reconnaissance aircraft. For the latter group this included the important need to ensure radio contact with forward air control vessels, who could then expediently respond to the valuable information that the reconnaissance aircraft provided. As in any such military action between opposing forces, the best laid plans rarely proceed as they are intended to.

In the planning for the raid, reconnaissance aircraft were allocated to undertake the following missions.

Tactical reconnaissance was to be made over the area of the operation, including the lines of approach of any enemy reinforcements, while coastal anti-surface vessel reconnaissance patrols were to be carried out between Cherbourg and Boulogne throughout the night prior to the raid itself.

Pilots on reconnaissance missions were in an extremely difficult position. Besides having to observe the fighting taking place on the land and sea below them, they also had to be aware of their own safety, making sure they had not been seen by, or were about to be attacked by, enemy aircraft. There was also the added complication and danger of enemy anti-aircraft fire, as well as ground smoke from fires, exploding shells and smoke bombs dropped and fired by the RAF and Royal Navy. The ability to be able to correctly interpret what it was they were seeing, along with providing the correct directions of those events, was an imperative requirement for the pilots.

The reconnaissance missions before and during the raid involved relaying back to the command vessel whether the attacking forces were progressing to their intended targets, or being beaten back by defending forces. The quicker the pilots were able to relay such information, the quicker real time amendments could be made. The missions also included the need to fly further inland, away from the actual fighting, to try to establish if any German reinforcements were making their way to Dieppe, and if they were, what type and how many there were.

If reconnaissance missions were to be effective, then the skies they were operating in needed to be as free of enemy aircraft as was possible. Besides having to take into account ground-based German anti-aircraft fire, there were also cases of gunners on board Royal Navy ships opening fire on RAF aircraft, having mistaken them for German ones. The extent of the danger for the pilots who flew the reconnaissance missions was highlighted when casualty figures were looked at in the aftermath of the raid. It was established that the tactical reconnaissance squadrons lost most aircraft and sustained the highest casualties. In the main this was due to the deep penetration into German-controlled territory that was required of the pilots who flew these missions, which necessitated their patrolling well beyond the area where fighter aircraft could cover. The coastal roads leading to Dieppe were reconnoitered every half an hour, whilst those from Amiens, Rouen, Yvetot and Le Harve, all other places from which reinforcements might be expected, were patrolled on an hourly basis.

The pilots took off from RAF Gatwick, flew across the English Channel to Dieppe, via Beachy Head, made contact with their command vessel, and were given their allotted targets via radio contact whilst they were still in the air. Having completed their missions, they made their way back to the area where the command vessel was located, and near enough to ensure that radio transmissions could be clearly heard and understood to ensure that any information they had to pass on was received without any misunderstanding. Once this was done, the reconnaissance aircraft were flown back to their base at Gatwick, where they relayed the information again, but this time to the Air Force Commander, by telephone.

One such pilot was Arnold George Christensen, who was born in Hastings, Hawkes Bay, New Zealand, on 8 April 1922 to parents Anton and Lilian Christensen. His father was Danish whilst his mother was a native New Zealander.

Prior to enlisting in the Royal New Zealand Air Force, Arnold had begun his working life in journalism working for the *Hawkes Bay Daily Mail* newspaper, but in June 1940, not long after his eighteenth birthday and determined to do his bit for the war effort, he applied to be a pilot. However, it would be another year before he was called up, possibly because it was felt that at 18, he was too young.

He began pilot training on 14 June 1941 at New Plymouth, on the west coast of New Zealand's North Island. There were no Spitfires for young Christensen to train in; for him it was a de Havilland Tiger Moth bi-plane, which was more akin to something from the First World War, even though it had first been designed and built in the 1930s. After four months of training in New Zealand, he was sent to Canada where he continued his training at the No. 4 Service Flying Training School at Saskatoon, Saskatchewan. His training went well, and after four months he had successfully completed his course and was a newly qualified service pilot. Soon after his arrival in England, he found himself posted to Old Sarum airfield, near Salisbury, home of the RAF's No. 41 Operational Training Unit. It was here that he qualified to become a fighter pilot and on 13 August 1942, he was posted to the RAF's No. 26 Squadron.

On 19 August, less than a week after he had been posted to No. 26 Squadron, Flight Lieutenant Christensen found himself flying an American Mustang Mark 1a, alongside his comrade, Pilot Officer E.E. O'Farrell, who was also in a Mustang aircraft. They were charged with carrying out a reconnaissance mission in support of the Dieppe Raid when both of their aircraft were struck by anti-aircraft fire. O'Farrell's plane quickly spun out of control and crashed into the sea, whilst Christensen managed to maintain control of his aircraft and began making his way back home. However, when barely halfway across the English Channel, his engine seized, leaving him no option but to land his Mustang in the sea as best he could. Once in the water, he clambered out of his cockpit, inflated and deployed his small dinghy, and waited to be rescued. Unfortunately for Christensen, not only did nobody come to his rescue, but the tides were against him, because instead of being swept back towards the white cliffs of Dover, after having spent two days adrift in the English Channel, he found himself being washed up on a French beach, straight into the arms of waiting German soldiers.

Christensen's time as a POW eventually saw him end up at Stalag Luft III, where he went on to become one of those who successfully escaped from the camp on the evening of Friday, 24 March 1944, but was sadly one of those who was subsequently caught and executed by the Nazis.

Christensen spoke both Danish and German. He and three other men, Norwegians Halldor Espelid and Nils Jørgen Fuglesang, and Australian James Catanach, who also spoke excellent German, initially stayed as a group of four before splitting up in the early stages of the escape. Christensen and Catanach caught a train to Berlin where they changed and picked up another that was heading to Hamburg. The pair then caught a third train and headed to the coastal town of Flensburg, close to the German-Danish border.

It was during this final leg of their journey that they were caught by German police officers on the train who had become suspicious of them. Unbeknown to Christensen and Catanach, Espelid and Fuglesang were also on the train and were also captured. When the train arrived in Flensburg, the four escapees were taken off and driven to the town's small prison. There they were handed over to Gestapo officers who, after interrogating them on 29 March 1944, told them they would be taken to a prison camp at Kiel, which was just over 50 miles away, a journey that would take about hour to complete. It was a journey that the four men never made. Instead, they were shot in a nearby field, execution style, with a bullet to the back of the head.

CHAPTER NINE

The Essex Scottish Regiment and the Rivait Brothers

The Canadian Essex Scottish Regiment was mobilised for war on 1 September 1939, with no shortage of men ready and willing to enlist to ensure that it was fully up to strength as quickly as possible. With the men of the regiment having completed their basic wartime training, they were fit and raring to go. They set sail for England as part of the 2nd Canadian Infantry Division on 16 August 1940, but having arrived it became a case of even more training. Dieppe would be their first taste of action, by which time the war was already three years old.

At dawn on 19 August, 553 members of the Essex Scottish Regiment landed at Red Beach in front of Dieppe. Between 03.30 and 03.40, 30 minutes after the initial landings, the main frontal assault by the Essex Scottish and the Royal Hamilton Light Infantry had begun. Both regiments were meant to be supported by Churchill tanks of the 14th Army Tank Regiment, who were supposed to be landing at the same time, but unfortunately, the tanks were late arriving on the beach. This resulted in the two infantry battalions having to carry out their attack without armoured support. A frontal assault on one of the town's most heavily defended sections was always going to be a difficult task, but without armoured support it was almost suicidal.

No sooner had the men of the Essex Scottish and the Royal Hamilton Light Infantry hit the heavily pebbled beach than they were met with heavy German machine gun fire from emplacements dug into the overlooking cliffs either side of the town's port, as well as those in buildings overlooking the seafront promenade. Unable to clear the obstacles and scale the adjacent seawall, the attacking men were like sitting ducks with little or nothing in the way of cover, resulting in both units sustaining heavy casualties.

At one point during the fighting, a small number of the regiment's men did manage to make their way off the beach and infiltrate the town, but this lead to a confusing message being received by General Roberts on board his headquarters ship located some miles out to sea. The initial message that a small number of men had managed to extricate themselves from the beach had somehow turned into the remaining contingent of men from the Essex Scottish making their way into the town and advancing. This led to General Roberts sending in his reserve battalion, Les Fusiliers Mont-Royal, who on landing on Red Beach immediately found themselves exposed to intense and accurate German machine gun fire, as they too became pinned down.

By 06.30 the battle was effectively over for the Essex Scottish and they were ordered to withdraw at 11.00. That was the easy part, but before they could escape, they had to make their way back across the beach to the waiting landing craft, all the time trying to avoid the German machine gun fire that was raining down on them. Only fifty-three men, some of whom were severely injured, reached safety and managed to return to England.

Three of the men who served with the Essex Scottish Regiment were the brothers Alphonse, Leon and Raymond Rivait, all of whom were from Windsor, Ontario, Canada. Alphonse, the youngest brother, who had been a truck driver before the war, enlisted in the Canadian Army on 3 July 1941. Leon, the eldest, who had worked as a car assembler, enlisted on 10 April 1940. Both were killed in action, whilst Raymond, who enlisted sometime between his two brothers, survived. Private Leon Rivait, who was 24 years of age when he died, is buried at the Dieppe Canadian War Cemetery at Hautot-sur-Mer. Sadly, the body of his 18-year-old brother, Private Alphonse Rivait, was never recovered. His name is commemorated on the Brookwood 1939-1945 Memorial in Surrey.

Meanwhile, 22-year-old Private Raymond Rivait was captured by the Germans and spent the rest of the war as a POW at Stalag II D, in north-west Poland. Upon his release at the end of the war, Raymond returned to his home in Windsor, and died, aged 70, on 30 June 1990. He is buried in the Heavenly Rest Catholic Cemetery in Windsor.

A fourth brother, Lawrence, was a private in the same regiment, and had enlisted in the Army on 16 September 1940. Like his brother Raymond, he was also a married man, who prior to enlisting had worked as a mechanic. Although he did not take part in the Dieppe Raid, he was killed in action on 23 November 1944 during fighting in the Netherlands.

Having already paid the painful price of losing three of their sons to the war, Homer and Bernadette Rivait petitioned the Canadian military authorities to get their other son, Edward, out of service. Although successful in their efforts in having him discharged, Edward was determined to do his bit and re-joined the Army a month later. Thankfully for his parents, the war was over before he had finished his basic training.

A newspaper article from the *Windsor Daily Star* dated 5 December 1944, featured the story of the Rivait brothers:

Windsor Mother's Third Son Reported Killed in Action

When two of Mrs Rivait's five soldier sons fell at Dieppe and a third was taken prisoner, she suffered a blow as great as any Canadian mother possibly could receive from this war and for over two years she had hoped that her remorse would be allayed by the safe return of her fourth boy serving overseas.

Serving in Reich

But that hope was shattered this week, when the mother who lives at 253 Belle Isle Street, Riverside, received word that her fourth son had been reported killed while serving in Germany.

Not many mothers have lost three sons in this war, but she is nevertheless grateful that her prisoner-of-war son is safe and will return home after this war is over.

The four brothers, Leon 25; Alphonse, 21, Raymond, 23, and Lawrence, 22, went overseas together three years ago with the Essex Scottish Regiment. Three of them went to Dieppe together, but none returned.

Leon and Alphonse paid the supreme sacrifice, while Raymond was taken prisoner.

The other brother, Lawrence, went into action for the first time this year and died in battle on November 23, according to word received this week. Another brother Edward, 18, is attached to an infantry unit stationed at Chatham.

CHAPTER TEN

Military Awards of the Dieppe Raid

As we have already seen in Chapter 3, Lieutenant Colonel Charles Merritt was the man in charge of the South Saskatchewan Regiment who landed on the beaches at Dieppe in the early hours of 19 August 1942.

Merritt was a career soldier, having entered Canada's Royal Military College at Kingston, Ontario, in 1925, when he was just 16 years of age. An outstanding student, at the end of his course he graduated with honours and was commissioned into the Militia Regiment of the Seaforth Highlanders of Canada. His instructors knew he would go on to become a caring and well-respected military leader.

A driven individual who was always looking for a new challenge, Merritt went on to study law and in 1932 became a barrister working out of Vancouver, a job he continued to do until the outbreak of war in Europe, which saw his mobilisation and promotion to the rank of major.

Christmas 1939 was his first away from his family, as by then he had already arrived in the UK to begin the journey that would see him awarded the highest Commonwealth military award for bravery in the face of the enemy.

In March 1942, having by then completed the War Staff Course at Camberley, Surrey, the home of military training for the British Army for nearly 200 years between 1802 and 1997, he was placed in command of the Canadian Army's South Saskatchewan Regiment, which by then had been decided would play an integral part in the raid on Dieppe. By May 1942, the regiment had moved to the Isle of Wight to begin its preparations for its date with destiny, although the regiment's men would not have been privy to the finite details of the journey they were about to undertake.

The main strike force at Dieppe was made up of British soldiers from the vastly experienced No. 3 and No. 4 Commandos, with the Canadians providing support on both flanks.

The main thrust of the attack was for British Commando units to attack and destroy German gun emplacements either side of the port of Dieppe. Their two drop off points had been designated White and Red beaches, immediately west of the town's port. As for the Canadian contingents, their main job was to form flank cover for the British troops to make sure they were not attacked from either side. The Royal Regiment of Canada and The Black Watch (Royal Highland Regiment) landed on what was designated as Blue Beach, whilst Merritt and his men of the South Saskatchewan Regiment, along with the Queen's Own Cameron Highlanders, landed on Green Beach, to the west of the port at Pourville.

The citation for Merritt's Victoria Cross appeared in the *London Gazette* newspaper of Friday, 2 October 1942. It read as follows:

Dieppe Raid, France, 19 August 1942, Lieutenant-Colonel Charles Cecil Merritt, Commanding Officer, South Saskatchewan Regiment, Canadian Infantry Corps.

For matchless gallantry and inspiring leadership whilst commanding his battalion during the Dieppe raid on the 19th August 1942. From the point of landing his unit's advance had to be made across a bridge in Pourville which was swept by very heavy machine gun, mortar and artillery fire, the first parties were mostly destroyed and the bridge thickly covered by their bodies. A daring lead was required: waving his helmet, Lieutenant Colonel Merritt rushed forward shouting "Come on over! There's nothing to worry about here". He thus personally led the survivors of at least four parties in turn across the bridge.

Quickly organizing these, he led them forward and when held up by enemy pillboxes he again headed rushes which succeeded in clearing them. In one case he himself destroyed the occupants of the post by throwing grenades into it. After several of his runners became casualties, he himself kept contact with his different positions.

Although twice wounded Lieutenant Colonel Merritt continued to direct the unit's operations with great vigour and determination and while organizing the withdrawal he stalked a sniper with a Bren gun and silenced him. He then coolly gave orders for the departure and announced his intention to hold off and "get even with" the enemy. When last seen he was collecting Bren and Tommy guns and preparing a defensive position which successfully covered the withdrawal from the beach.

Lieutenant Colonel Merritt is now reported to be a Prisoner of War. To this Commanding Officer's personal daring, the success of his unit's operations and the safe re-embarkation of a large portion of it were chiefly due.

By the time the Dieppe Raid was over and the fighting had stopped, eighty-four of Merritt's men had been killed, while a further eighty-nine, including himself, had been captured. After having his wounds treated, he found himself incarcerated in the German prisoner of War camp for officers, Oflag VII-B, at Eichstatt, Bavaria, some 60 miles north of Munich, where he arrived on 31 August 1942.

Together with sixty-four others, he escaped from his enforced incarceration via a 120-foot long tunnel during the night of 3/4 June 1943. After a massive manhunt, all of the escapees, including Merritt, were recaptured, and he was sentenced to fourteen days' solitary confinement. On completion, he was transferred to Oflag IV-C at Colditz Castle. After being freed at the end of the war he commented: 'My war lasted six hours. There are plenty of Canadians who went all the way from the landings in Sicily to the very end.'

It would appear from his comments that he felt slightly ill at ease about the awarding of his Victoria Cross, especially when measured against fellow Canadian comrades who had seen years of active service, whilst he saw out the war in the comparative luxury of an officers' POW camp. There was another aspect to Merritt's award of the VC, in so far as it was unusual for any gallantry medal, including the VC, to be given to any member of the military who had been captured by the enemy and become a POW.

Charles Merritt received his Victoria Cross at Buckingham Palace from King George VI on 22 June 1945. His achievement was even more notable for the fact that in receiving his award, he became the first Canadian to do so in the European theatre of war.

The next man to be awarded the Victoria Cross was Major Patrick Anthony Porteous of the Royal Regiment of Artillery, who had received his commission with the regiment in 1937 as a second lieutenant. On 26 August 1940 he was promoted to the rank of lieutenant, before being further promoted to the rank of captain on 19 August 1942. By the time of the raid on Dieppe, Porteous was 24 years old and held the rank of temporary major. He was attached to No. 4 Commando when he carried out the actions for which he was awarded the VC.

No. 4 Commando's part in the raid was to take out the Hess battery, which was situated on the western side of the town and consisted of six 150-mm (5.9 inch) guns, fortified in a concrete emplacement some 1,100 yards inland. The emplacement was heavily defended, being surrounded by two rows of barbed wire, and further protected by several machine gun teams. In addition, a nearby anti-aircraft tower could also provide defence against a ground attack. The men of No. 4 Commando had been responsible for their own planning for the operation and had selected two landing beaches, codenamed Orange One and Two. Orange One Beach, which was situated at Varengeville, was overlooked by a chalk cliff. Before the war there had been steps leading down to the beach, but these had been removed in case of a possible invasion and replaced with barbed wire, while further obstacles made it an unattractive proposition for an attacking enemy force.

Orange Two was at Quiberville, more than a mile further west at the mouth of the River Saâne. This offered access to the top of the cliffs but was protected by two German machine gun pillboxes, as well as barbed wire, and was further away from their target. Intelligence reports had estimated the strength of the battery they were about to attack was somewhere in the region of 150 men, with a further two infantry companies stationed nearby who could be called upon when needed.

The plan was for No. 4 Commando to be split into two groups, one of which was under the command of Major Mills-Roberts, who landed on Orange One, with the other under the command of Lieutenant Colonel Lovat, who landed on Orange Two. The Mills-Roberts group blew their way through barbed wire defences with the use of two Bangalore torpedoes, thus allowing them to scale the cliffs to land in front of the battery, whilst Lovat's group took a longer route, bringing them to the rear of the battery. Another section of men were left to guard the beach area to ensure the withdrawal went smoothly. Major Porteous was with F Troop (part of Mills-Roberts' group) and it was his job to act as the liaison officer between the two attacking units.

When the assault started at 06.15, F Troop discovered a group of Germans, and after charging into them, they were dispersed without loss to the Commandos. The troop continued their advance, moving between buildings and an orchard, when they were themselves caught in the open by heavy gun fire. The two men at the head of the troop, commander Captain Pettiward and Lieutenant McDonald, were killed, whilst Troop Sergeant Major Stockdale was wounded. It was during this action that the already wounded Captain Porteous, was awarded the Victoria Cross.

At 06.30 a flare fired by Lovat signalled the start of the assault. Group one ceased firing and B and F troops charged the battery with fixed bayonets. The objective for B Troop was the battery buildings, while F Troop targeted the guns. Captain Porteous, who was now commanding F Troop, was again wounded, this time by a bullet to the thigh, but he still managed to urge his men on. He was shot for a third time and passed out just as the battery was captured. Demolition experts from F Troop placed explosive charges in and around the battery to destroy it.

Carrying their wounded, including Captain Porteous and a number of German prisoners, both troops withdrew back towards the beach. Still in contact with the Germans, both groups of Commandos eventually made it to Orange One, where they were rescued at 08.15 by landing craft vessels. They then crossed the English Channel without further incident, arriving at Newhaven docks at 14.45 later that day.

Despite having sustained a number of wounds, Captain Porteous went on to make a full recovery and had a long and distinguished military career, serving in Palestine, Germany and Singapore. Following the war he was promoted to captain, and promoted again to the rank of major in 1950. He became a lieutenant colonel on 1 May 1959 and finished his military career in 1970 with the rank of colonel. He had the honour of being in the leading car at the late Queen Mother's 100th birthday parade, and died in October 2000 at the age of 82.

The citation for his Victoria Cross also appeared in the *London Gazette* of Friday 2 October:

The King has been graciously pleased to approve the award of The VICTORIA CROSS to:- Captain (temporary Major) Anthony Patrick Porteous (73033) Royal Regiment of Artillery (Fleet, Hants.).

At Dieppe on the 19th August 1942, Major Porteous was detailed to act as a Liaison Officer between the two detachments whose task was to assault the heavy coast defence guns.

In the initial assault Major Porteous, working with the smaller of the two detachments, was shot at close range through the hand, the bullet passing through his palm and entering his upper arm. Undaunted Major Porteous closed with his assailant, succeeded in disarming him and killed him with his own bayonet thereby saving the life of a British Sergeant on whom the Germans had turned their aim.

In the meantime the larger detachment was held up, and the officer leading this attachment was killed and the Troop Sergeant-Major fell seriously wounded. Almost immediately afterwards the only other officer of the detachment was also killed.

Major Porteous, without hesitation and in the face of a withering enemy fire, dashed across the open ground to take over the command of this detachment. Rallying them, he led them in a charge which carried the German position at the point of the bayonet and was severely wounded for the second time. Though shot through the thigh he continued to the final objective where he eventually collapsed from loss of blood after the last of the guns had been destroyed.

Major Porteous's most gallant conduct, his brilliant leadership and tenacious devotion to a duty which was supplementary to the role originally assigned to him, was an inspiration to the whole detachment.

The third Victoria Cross awarded for actions undertaken during the Dieppe Raid appeared in the pages of the *London Gazette* on Tuesday, 14 February 1946, and was made by the Canadian Department of National Defence in Ottawa. The man in question was Honorary Captain John Weir Foote. The citation for his award was as follows:

The King has been graciously pleased to approve the award of the Victoria Cross to:- Honorary Captain John Weir Foote, Canadian Chaplain Services.

At Dieppe, on 19th August 1942, Honorary Captain Foote, Canadian Chaplain Services, was Regimental Chaplain with the Royal Hamilton Light Infantry.

Upon landing on the beach under heavy fire he attached himself to the Regimental Aid Post which had been set up in a slight depression on the beach, but which was only sufficient to give cover to men lying down. During the subsequent period of eight hours, while the action continued, this officer not only assisted the Regimental Medical Officer in ministering to the wounded in the Regimental Aid Post, but time and again left this shelter to inject morphine, give first aid and carry wounded personnel from the open beach to the Regimental Aid Post. On these occasions, with utter disregard for his personal safety, Honorary Captain Foote exposed himself to an inferno of fire and saved many lives by his gallant efforts.

During the action, as the tide went out, the Regimental Aid Post was moved to the shelter of a stranded landing craft. Honorary Captain Foote continued tirelessly and courageously to carry wounded men from the exposed beach to the cover of the landing craft. He also removed wounded from inside the landing craft when ammunition had been set on fire by enemy shells. When landing craft appeared he carried wounded from the Regimental Aid Post to the landing craft through very heavy fire.

On several occasions this officer had the opportunity to embark but returned to the beach as his chief concern was the care and evacuation of the wounded. He refused a final opportunity to leave the shore, choosing to suffer the fate of the men he had ministered to for over three years.

Honorary Captain Foote personally saved many lives by his efforts and his example inspired all around him. Those who observed him, state that the calmness of this heroic officer as he walked about, collecting the wounded on the fire swept beach will never be forgotten.

John Foote had begun his life in the Presbyterian priesthood in 1934, but despite his chosen path in life, once war had broken out in Europe, and Canadians were being sent to help their Commonwealth cousins, he did not hesitate to enlist in the Canadian Chaplain's Corps, which he did in December 1939. He was posted to the Royal Hamilton Light Infantry (Wentworth Regiment) as their chaplain and given the rank of honorary captain. When the regiment's 1st Battalion was sent to England in July 1940, Foote went with them.

Although not unheard of, it was very unusual for an Army chaplain to go in to battle, especially as being a non-combatant meant he would not have been allowed to carry a weapon. However, on 19 August 1942, Foote stood shoulder-to-shoulder alongside the very men to whom he provided religious comfort and guidance, and stepped off the landing craft with them onto the beaches of Dieppe in the face of heavy enemy fire. That was brave enough, but the citation for the award of his Victoria Cross provided the true extent of the man's bravery.

Along with the wounded men of his regiment, Captain Foote was captured at Dieppe and spent the following three years in captivity as a prisoner of war, despite the fact that he had had every opportunity to board one of the landing craft and escape. Instead, he chose to stay behind so that he could be of assistance to the men of his regiment and the other Canadians on the beach who were also wounded.

Foote was presented with his Victoria Cross by King George VI at Buckingham Palace on 28 March 1946. After returning to Canada, he remained with the Royal Canadian Army Chaplain Corps until he was demobbed in 1948.

The only question that remains about John Foote is why the awarding of his Victoria Cross was not announced until 1946, when Charles Merritt, who was also captured at Dieppe, had his Victoria Cross announced in 1942. It can only be assumed that the extent of his actions did not come to official notice until after the release of other Canadian POWs from the Dieppe Raid.

One aspect of the Dieppe Raid that is quite staggering is the number of honours and awards that were issued, especially when considering it was a failed operation which lasted just ten hours.

In total, out of the approximate 10,500 men who took part in the operation, 511 such awards were handed out, meaning that roughly one in twenty of those involved was officially honoured. These awards ranged from being Mentioned in Despatches, to the Victoria Cross, and also included the Distinguished Flying Medal, the Military Medal, the Distinguished Service Medal, the Conspicuous Gallantry Medal, the Distinguished Flying Cross, Bar to the Distinguished Flying Cross, Military Cross, Bar to the Military Cross, the Distinguished Service Cross, Member of the British Empire, the Distinguished Service Order, Bar to the Distinguished Service Order, and the Order of the British Empire.

One example of these awards was Ordinary Seaman Thomas Albert Lee, who was awarded the Conspicuous Gallantry Medal (CGM) for his actions. The citation for his award appeared in the *London Gazette* of Friday, 2 October 1942 and read as follows:

> While the craft in which Ordinary Seaman Lee was serving was beached for some fifteen minutes, landing tanks, under concentrated fire, her guns were kept in action against an enemy gun position and houses on the beach until all the gun crews had been killed or wounded. Although gravely injured himself, his

cheerful courage and devotion to duty were an example to the rest. He carried on until the guns were silenced and then crawled away to report to his skipper.

The CGM was only second to the Victoria Cross in awards given for bravery and had first been established in 1855 during the Crimean War. Although originally only intended for ratings in the Royal Navy, in April 1940 this was extended to include those serving in the RAF, while members of the British Army were also included from July 1942 if serving aboard a ship. In September 1940, ratings in the Merchant Navy were also deemed eligible to receive it.

Lieutenant John Edward Rogers Wood of the Canadian Royal Engineers was awarded the Military Cross for his actions at Dieppe. The citation for his award read as follows:

> During the raid on Dieppe, 19 August 1942, Lieutenant Wood was aboard a landing craft which beached some 50 feet from shore. He swam ashore and returned to the ship several times through heavy fire, assisting aboard the wounded who had attempted to land. This officer was in the water some considerable time, and although wounded himself, displayed marked leadership in the rescue of the wounded, and with no regard for himself, carried on throughout the entire action, undoubtedly saving many lives. When the tide receded, Lieutenant Wood unloaded and carried ashore behive charges for engineer demolitions and rolls of tracking for tanks. At this time the landing craft had been hit and was burning. He carried on his work in the open under intense enemy fire without thought for his own

safety. He showed remarkable coolness in handling men and was a splendid example to us all.

As in all military actions, acts of bravery are carried out by a number of individuals. Sometimes these acts go unreported for a number of reasons, sometimes it is difficult to understand the decision making process behind who was awarded what. A good example of this was the Mentioned in Despatches award given to Company Sergeant Major William Jacobs. Here is the citation for his award:

> Warrant Officer II William Stewart Milford Jacobs (Royal Regiment of Canada). While in command of the Royal Regiment of Canada battalion headquarters protective detachtment at Dieppe, 19 August 1942, Company Sergeant Major Jacobs led his men to the sea wall. Noticing that a landing craft filled with wounded men was attempting to back off the beach while under heavy fire from a pillbox, he left the comparative safety of the sea wall and, going out into the open, threw his grenades at the vision slits of the pillbox, disrupting the aim of the garrison. Having exhausted his supply of grenades, he called to his men to toss him more, and these he continued to throw until killed by enemy light automatic fire.

This story highlights the finite margins in decisions which determine what gallantry award, if any, a man was given for his acts of bravery. It could be easily argued that Jacobs' actions merited a Victoria Cross.

Another award that merits a mention is the one given to Private Gerard Cloutier of Les Fusiliers Mont-Royal, who was killed in action during the course of the raid. He was Mentioned in Despatches (MID) for his part in the raid which went some way in highlighting the disparity in the reasoning and decision making behind the giving of such awards. It should be remembered that at the time of Cloutier's death, the only gallantry awards that could be issued posthumously were the Victoria Cross, George Cross and being Mentioned in Despatches.

During the raid, and whilst performing the duties of an officer's batman, Cloutier crossed the beach on more than one occasion to make contact with battalion headquarters after his company commander had lost communications which prevented him from receiving further instructions. On each occasion he placed himself in extreme danger and displayed bravery, heroism and extreme courage in the face of the enemy, all whilst under almost constant enemy fire. He also assisted in giving first aid to wounded colleagues at his position. When on the receiving end of a sustained burst of German machine gun fire, his company commander was wounded and without thinking, Cloutier threw himself over the officer to protect him from sustaining any further injury. In doing so, however, he was immediately mortally wounded. Why Cloutier's actions only warranted being Mentioned in Despatches and not a Victoria Cross, remains an absolute mystery.

CHAPTER ELEVEN

The German Perception of the Raid

❖

The Allied raid on Dieppe would have no doubt been confusing for the Germans. After all, they had no advance knowledge that it would take place, being vastly different in scope and extent to any previous amphibious operations carried out by British and Allied forces.

The strength of the raiding party was far greater than it had been on any previous occasion, when Commando raids had been undertaken against nominated targets along the German-occupied European coastline, such as Operation Biting, also known as the Bruneval Raid, which took place in February 1942 and consisted of an actual raiding party of just 120 officers and men.

The Dieppe Raid was different in that it was the first time one had been carried out during the early hours of the morning, and it was also the first time tanks as well as troops attempted to land.

The BBC radio announcement made the night before the raid provided information about such an event taking place, highlighting the fact that this was not a full-scale invasion, but simply a raid. However, the message failed to name an exact location where the raiding troops would come ashore. There is no doubt that the German authorities would have also listened in to that same transmission. Consequently, the dilemma for them was whether they took it at face value, or believed it was simply a bluff on the part of the British authorities.

For the local German military commanders in charge of the region around Dieppe, the question was how to respond to such a raid. If they simply ignored the radio transmission and did nothing, they would look rather foolish if Dieppe was the intended target, as it subsequently was, especially if it then turned out to be a full-scale invasion. They would then quickly have had to consider whether they had enough troops at Dieppe, and if so, were they placed at the right locations and in sufficient numbers? Other considerations would include ensuring the right means of transport were available to them and to what degree, if any, would Allied aircraft cause damage to the road and railways in and around Dieppe?

This was the same issue faced by all German military commanders along the entire length of the French coastline, meaning that any of them even thinking of requesting reinforcements or additional military hardware, such as tanks, had to be mindful that they simply may not be available.

Having listened to the BBC message, the other dilemma faced by the German defenders was how long did they hold their positions for before they 'stood down'. A day, two days, a week, or even longer? There was simply no clue to where or when the raid would take place. For the German commanders it really more a question of 'what if?' or 'dammed if they did and damned if they didn't'.

The best weapon the Germans had at their disposal to deal with the situation was intelligence. If the information they had on a potential raid was correct and up to date, then they could afford to take certain risks. But if it turned out to be incorrect, then the actions taken and decisions made could turn out to be catastrophic for the German soldiers on the ground.

The European coastline to be defended was nearly 400 miles in length, meaning it was a logistical nightmare for German commanders. The coastline was split into various sectors, with each area allocated a number of men to guard beaches and seafronts, backed up by reserve forces stationed nearby.

In early 1942, German manpower was at a premium. In France and the low countries, Germany had somewhere in the region of thirty divisions, or approximately 360,000 men, in addition to coastal defence troops, but this meant that any reserves would not have been substantial enough. For such reserves to then be utilised was not a straight-forward matter, as the Army commander in charge of the Dieppe area would have had to take into account the size of the attacking Allied force, whilst at the same time trying to determine what he was actually up against. Was it a raid or a full-size invasion force? Part of his thinking would have included the knowledge that Dieppe was not of any real military importance or significance.

What undoubtedly would have concerned the German defenders was the appearance of tanks on the beaches of Dieppe. This concern would have been two-fold. Firstly, no other raid carried out by the Allies up to that point in the war had ever included the use of tanks, and secondly, the Germans did not have large, armoured forces in place at Dieppe.

By not knowing what he was up against, the German commander at Dieppe, Field Marshal Gerd von Rundstedt, had the difficult decision to make about whether he should send reserve units to Dieppe, knowing full well that if he did, these would have to come from those ear-marked for the Cherbourg peninsula, which militarily was a much more strategic location than Dieppe. Part of any decision-making process would have undoubtedly included the fact that drawing reserves intended for Cherbourg might be exactly what the British were hoping for, and what the raid was actually all about, and thus Cherbourg would be left vulnerable.

Besides the intentions of the attacking force and whether to call up reserves, what about the local French population? Would they rise-up in revolt, despite the radio transmission by the BBC asking them not to? If they did, the commander would potentially have to deal with acts of sabotage, the killing of his troops, the destruction of supplies, signals, communications, roads, railways, bridges, and petrol and ammunition centres.

Such confusions and uncertainties, despite any actual damage or deaths which may or may not occur, were in part the exact purpose of what Commando raids were designed to produce.

The German people were told of the raid on the evening of 19 August by way of a special bulletin released by the High Command of the German Armed Forces (OKW). It explained that Allied forces had landed at Dieppe, with their main intention being 'to form a bridgehead around Dieppe'. It also told how German forces had repelled the raid and, in doing so, had 'inflicted heavy casualties on the enemy'. The bulletin concluded by saying, 'The enemy has suffered a decisive defeat. His attempt at invasion served only political purposes and was contrary to all military common sense.'

The reference to 'political purposes' no doubt concerned their belief that Churchill's motive for the attack was for no other reason than to appease Stalin, to whom he had previously made a promise about the opening up of a second front.

Besides being a victory for Germany, Dieppe also provided Reich Minister Joseph Goebbels and his department with enormous amounts of valuable and positive propaganda with which to bombard the German people. Although Hitler knew full well that Dieppe was not a serious attempt at opening up a second front, it more than suited his purpose to allow the German people to believe that it had been. This not only helped to sustain their morale, but it went a long way to maintaining their support for the continuation of the war.

Hitler was not just happy with the efforts of his men stationed at the coastal garrison at Dieppe, but also with the subsequent and extended propaganda made of it by Goebbels and his team.

Ultimately, both sides had learned from the events at Dieppe and despite having clearly been a German victory, positives could be taken by all. Sometime in late September 1942, Hitler met with his leading western based commanders at his headquarters in the Ukraine, where he told them, 'The next invasion attempt in the West will rely far more on-air power. We must realise that we are not alone in learning a lesson from Dieppe. The British have also learned. We must reckon with a totally different mode of attack and at quite a different place.' To this he added that, 'continued vigilance along the Atlantic Wall now had a vital role'. Nevertheless, he finished with the somewhat naïve comment: 'If nothing happens in the next year, we have won the war.'

CHAPTER TWELVE

The Dieppe Raid in the News

On Wednesday, 19 August 1942, two communiques were released by the Combined Operations Headquarters. The first was released at 06.45:

> A raid was launched in the early hours of today on the Dieppe area of enemy occupied France. The operation is still in progress, and a further communique will be issued when fuller reports are available.
>
> Meanwhile the French people are being advised by wireless broadcasts that this raid is not an invasion.

The warning to the people of France broadcast in French by the BBC throughout the night read:

> We urge the people of all regions concerned to avoid any action which might compromise their security. When the day comes to ask the active help of the French people, we will say so. We have promised to

do so, and we will keep our promise. Today we say to you, 'Do nothing. Do not expose yourselves to German reprisals. France and her Allies will need you on the day of Liberation.'

British authorities had to be extremely careful with their radio broadcast so as not to give any clue about where the raid was going to take place, just in case the Germans managed to work out where it would be. At the same time, they need to let the civilian population know that wherever the raid was taking place, it was not the main invasion they had been waiting for.

The second communique released by the Combined Operations Headquarters came at 13.00 the same day:

> The troops taking part in the raid on the Dieppe area have landed at all the points selected. Heavy opposition was encountered in some places, and on the left flank one landing party was initially repulsed, but reformed, and later carried the beach by assault. The troops on the right flank, having achieved their objective, which included the complete destruction of a six gun battery and ammunition dump, have now been re-embarked. In the centre tanks were landed and heavy fighting is proceeding.
>
> The military force consists mainly of Canadian troops. Also taking part are British Special Troops (commandos), a detachment from a US Ranger battalion, and a small contingent of Fighting French. This force was carried and escorted by units of the Royal Navy. Air support and protection on a large scale is being provided by bomber and fighter

aircraft of the RAF, in the face of considerable enemy opposition.

A further communique will be issued later.

Despite these communications from the British authorities, the American authorities decided to make their own announcement concerning their involvement in the day's events at Dieppe. The following communique was released by the US Headquarters located somewhere in the south of England: 'In the combined operations raid on the Dieppe area today, a detachment from the US Ranger Battalion is taking part with Canadian forces, British Special Service Troops, and a small detachment of the Fighting French.'

This was followed later the same day by a further announcement by the Americans:

> Specially selected American task troops chosen from amongst an avalanche of volunteers from various branches of the Army, have been in training for some time with the commandos, headed by Vice-Admiral Louis Mountbatten, Chief of Combined Operations. These special task troops in training at certain commando depots somewhere in the United Kingdom, make up what are known as the United States Ranger Battalions.

> United States officers have for some time been serving on the staff of the Chief of Combined Operations, Vice-Admiral Louis Mountbatten. They have been serving as planners and advisers, alongside officer of the British Navy, Army and the Royal Air Force.

It was extremely unusual for British military authorities to make such announcements. In many cases it would be days or even weeks after an event had taken place before any announcement, or an acknowledgement of the facts, would even be considered. Yet here were Combined Operations almost providing a running commentary of the raid on Dieppe. Looking at it by today's standards, and with numerous available social media platforms, it appears somewhat bizarre. It is unclear as to the intention or purpose of these communiques. In today's world, where events are often captured and relayed for general consumption in real time thanks to modern technology, it would be understandable for such communiques to be released as they would readily provide official clarification and clear up any confusion or uncertainty. However, the raid on Dieppe was carried out in an era where this was not possible, so their purpose remains a mystery. Despite this, the communiques kept coming.

At an unspecified time in the late afternoon of 19 August 1942, the Combined Operations HQ released the following communique:

> Despite the clear statement issued in our first communique at six o'clock this morning and broadcast to the French at 6.15am, about the raid on Dieppe, German propaganda, unable to make other capital out of the turn the operations have taken, claimed that the raid was an invasion raid they have frustrated.
>
> In fact, the re-embarkation of the main forces engaged was begun six minutes after the time scheduled, and it has been completed nine hours after the initial

landing as planned. Some tanks have been lost during the action ashore, and reports show that fighting has been very fierce and that casualties are likely to have been heavy on both sides. Full reports will not be available until our forces are back in England.

In addition to the destruction of the six-gun battery, an ammunition dump, reported in our earlier communique, a radiolocation station, and a Flak battery were destroyed.

It is quite remarkable to remember that all the communiques released were done so on the very day that the events unfolded. This was almost unprecedented at this point in the war, and for the families back in the UK, who by chance happened to know what their loved ones were up to, it must have been an extremely traumatic time.

The communique continued:

Our new tank landing craft were in action today for the first time. There was intense activity by aircraft of all Operation Commands of the R.A.F. in support of the landing of our troops against the heavy enemy defences, and air fighting on the most intense scale also developed. From reports so far, 72 enemy aircraft are known to have been destroyed, in addition to a number of shot down by naval vessels. More than 100 enemy aircraft were also probably destroyed or damaged. Ninety-five of all Commands are missing, but 21 fighter pilots are known to be safe, and it is thought that others will prove to have been rescued.

One of the earliest articles to appear in the Press about the Dieppe Raid was a detailed account in *The Scotsman* on Thursday, 20 August 1942:

Dieppe Raid Completed to Schedule
Vital experience Gained for Invasion
Tank-Landing Craft in Action
95 Allied Aircraft Lost; 82 Germans Destroyed

Nine hours after landing in the Dieppe area at dawn yesterday, the main Allied forces had been re-embarked, and the latest raid on France was complete.

Combined Operations Headquarters reports that fighting has been very fierce, and that casualties are likely to have been heavy on both sides.

Apart from losses inflicted on the enemy, "vital experience" has been gained in the employment of substantial numbers of troops in an assault, and in the transport and use of heavy equipment during combined operations. Our new tank-landing craft were in action for the first time.

American, Canadian, and British aircraft gave support to the troops, and 95 are missing. Twenty-one fighter pilots are safe. Eighty-two German aircraft were destroyed, and more than that number probably destroyed or damaged.

Return of the Landing Party
Transport by Power-Driven Sea-Going
Barges

A number of the Commandos taking part in the raid arrived back in this country last evening, after taking part in the biggest raid yet launched on enemy-occupied territory. It was the first occasion on which Allied tanks had been in action on the Continent since the evacuation of Dunkirk.

The men landed at a southern port, from power-driven sea going barges, and were transferred to lorries which drove off from the harbour without delay. They were grimy and tired, but cheerful and singing.

Fourteen trucks and three motor coaches took them away. Hospital trains arrived for the wounded.

On the Commandos' faces were the remains of black, green or yellow paint. All wore balaclava helmets, and most had sand shoes, but others wore Army boots. One man walked barefooted along the street carrying his boots in his hands. Several had lost a trouser leg below the knee.

The Lost Cup

There was a little delay while the men entered the trucks and motor coaches, but it was long enough for some of the cottagers to run indoors and reappear with cups of tea, matches and cigarettes. One coach went off so quickly that a Commando had no time to return a cup. The woman looked glum for a moment. Then she cheerfully said: "Well, he's worth it."

The men carried rifles. Each had a deflated lifebelt across his chest.

"Good show boys," called waiting Canadian transport drivers, as the men marched from the dock gates. "Glad you made it."

A man who had made his third Commando raid said: "It was the hottest I have been in."

The detailed description about the returning Commandos is extremely interesting. What the article did not clarify, however, was whether it came from a newspaper reporter who was present at the port where the returning men were arriving, or from an official source who had informed the Press about the circumstances of their return.

The article continues to say:

Canadians Provide Transport

Preparations began early in the afternoon at a South Coast port (Newhaven, East Sussex) for the return of men taking part. Nearly all the transport was provided by Canadians. Lines of trucks, station wagons, and a number of ambulances, marshalled by members of the Royal Canadian Mounted Police on high-powered motor cycles, converged on the docks. In addition, single deck motor coaches were driven by members of a British unit.

A few of the ambulances were passed through the dock gates. Others covered with camouflage netting, were parked on the roadside. The remaining transport was lined up in the side streets.

All too often the aftermath of such an event is never described in such detail, possibly because the main interest is in the raid itself, along with the actions and bravery of those individuals who took part in it. The focus, more often than not, is whether or not the outcome of the raid was an Allied victory or defeat. How many men were killed and wounded, losses of vehicles, vessels and aircraft, and who, if anyone, received military awards for individual acts of bravery. How a man looked on his return, whether he was wounded, and whether he was offered a cup of tea and some cigarettes, pails into insignificance when compared to the overall picture of the raid.

The article continues:

> About 4 pm a tug came into the harbour, and soon afterwards an ambulance containing men with their legs bound in splints, sped away from the dock to a hospital in a nearby town.
>
> It was followed soon afterwards by a small truck filled with men.

Forces Engaged

Those involved in the raid were a combination of British, Canadian, Americans and Free French forces who were deployed in the landing. Carried

DISCOVER MORE ABOUT PEN & SWORD BOOKS

Pen & Sword Books have over 4000 books currently available, our imprints include: Aviation, Naval, Military, Archaeology, Transport, Frontline, Seaforth and the Battleground series, and we cover all periods of history on land, sea and air.

Can we stay in touch? From time to time we'd like to send you our latest catalogues, promotions and special offers by post. If you would prefer not to receive these, please tick this box. ❏

We also think you'd enjoy some of the latest products and offers by post from our trusted partners: companies operating in the clothing, collectables, food & wine, gardening, gadgets & entertainment, health & beauty, household goods, and home interiors categories. If you would like to receive these by post, please tick this box. ❏

We respect your privacy. We use personal information you provide us with to send you information about our products, maintain records and for marketing purposes. For more information explaining how we use your information please see our privacy policy at www.pen-and-sword.co.uk/privacy. You can opt out of our mailing list at any time via our website or by calling 01226 734222.

Mr/Mrs/Ms ....

Address... Email address...............................

Postcode.............................

Website: www.pen-and-sword.co.uk Email: enquiries@pen-and-sword.co.uk
Telephone: 01226 734555 Fax: 01226 734438
Stay in touch: facebook.com/penandswordbooks or follow us on Twitter @penswordbooks

Freepost Plus RTKE-RGRJ-KTTX
Pen & Sword Books Ltd
47 Church Street
BARNSLEY
S70 2AS

Lord Louis Mountbatten, Chief of Combined Operations and the architect of the raid on Dieppe.

Generaloberst Curt Haase, German 15th Army, the man in charge of Channel coastal defences from possible Allied invasion.

British Commandos training for the raid on Dieppe in Achnacarry, Scotland.

HMS *Berkeley* was involved in the Allied landings at Dieppe.

Canadians prepare to make their way to the beach at Dieppe.

Left: RAF Sergeant Jack Nissenthall, the British radar expert who undertook a secret mission during the raid. He was not to be captured at any cost and was provided with a cyanide capsule and a bodyguard of twelve men who had orders to shoot him if it appeared he was about to be taken prisoner.

Below: Dead Canadian soldiers cover the beach at Dieppe.

Above left: Lieutenant Edward Loustalot of the 1st Ranger Battalion was the first American killed at Dieppe.

Above right: Lieutenant Joseph Randall, one of the first three American Rangers killed at Dieppe.

Dead Canadian soldiers, a landing craft and tanks on the beach at Dieppe.

Left: Lieutenant Colonel Charles Merritt was captured at Dieppe and later awarded the Victoria Cross.

Below and opposite: Captured Canadian soldiers at Dieppe.

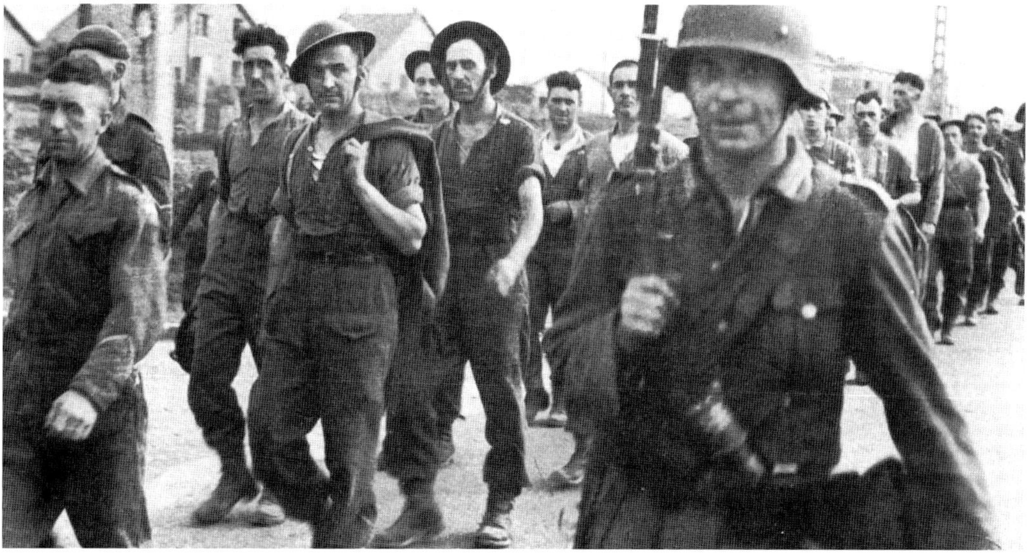

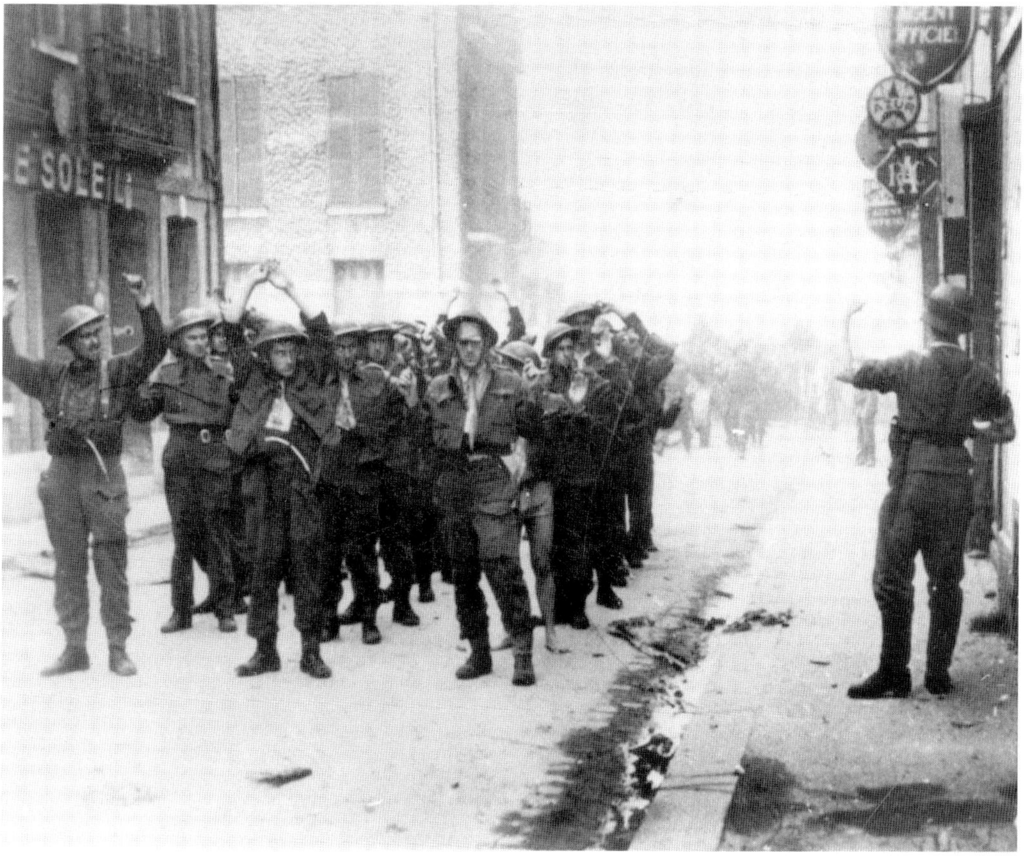

Captured Canadian tank and soldiers.

Makeshift hospital for wounded Canadian POWs guarded by German soldiers.

Right: A German defender at Dieppe posing in front of a captured Canadian tank.

Below: German soldiers inspect a captured Canadian tank.

German officer and soldier pose for a photograph sat on top of a captured Canadian tank.

Abandoned Canadian vehicles on the beach at Dieppe.

A knocked-out tank being examined by a German soldier.

Canadian soldiers being rescued from the beach at Dieppe.

Landing craft returning to a Royal Navy vessel at the end of the raid.

British Commandos returning to England after the raid.

Above: Allied soldiers arrive back at an English port after the raid.

Right: A Brigadier chats with wounded Canadian soldiers on their return from Dieppe.

Wounded Canadian soldiers returning to England after the raid.

Members of No. 3 Commando returning to Newhaven.

VICTIMES CIVILES

BASLY Alexandre	29 ans	GODALIER Sénateur	52 ans
BEZIRAD Marie épouse Menival	46 ans	GODÉ Fernand	31 ans
BIDARD Jean	22 ans	GORCE Jean	18 ans
BOUVIER Cécile	8 ans	GOYE Suzanne épouse Boucourt	55 ans
BRUNET Lucienne	25 ans	GROUT Arthur	50 ans
BRUNET Roger	16 ans	GUENO Pierre	7 ans
BRUNET Suzanne épouse Carpentier	23 ans	HURAY Marcel	15 ans
BUREAU Angèle épouse Davenet	59 ans	HURAY Raymond	15 ans
CASTELIN Aristide	70 ans	HUREL Emile	49 ans
CLAIRE Louis	89 ans	LEMARCHAND Madeleine épouse Burette	52 ans
CLERMONT Louise	19 ans	LEQUIEN Louis	37 ans
CONSEIL André	37 ans	LEROUX Fernand	37 ans
COUSIN Henri	55 ans	LEVASSEUR Paul	54 ans
DEBONNE Eugénie épouse Folliot	55 ans	LORPHELIN Marcel	22 ans
DE HAYES Auguste	56 ans	MAGNIER Marguerite	20 ans
DE HAYES Edouard	50 ans	MAGNIER André	16 ans
DUVAL Yvonne épouse Bosquier	29 ans	MAGNIER Charles	50 ans
ELLUIN Albertine épouse Siour	39 ans	MENIVAL Bernard	13 ans
FREVILLE Claude	3 ans	PEGARD Albertine	17 ans
GAILLARDON Charles	17 ans	SAMSON Albert	38 ans
GALLENE René	22 ans	SAUTREL Jean	16 ans
GAUTIER Clémence épouse Meunier	51 ans	VEREL Alban	46 ans
GIFFARD Gabrielle épouse Morin	44 ans	YING PONG Sui	51 ans

Lors du raid du 19 août 1942, 46 civils ont péri parmi la population de la région.
Treize d'entre eux avaient moins de vingt ans.
Ne les oublions pas.

List of French civilians killed during the raid on Dieppe.

German soldiers burying their dead after the raid was over.

Commando memorial at Spean Bridge, Scotland.

> and escorted by the Navy, they had been given large-scale protection by the RAF.
>
> Some of the Frenchmen were fighting within a few miles of their own homes. They were all exceptional physical types, who have received the special training given to British Commandos, and have seen fighting in half a dozen theatres of war.
>
> The main body of the landing force was composed of Canadians, but these constituted only about a third of the personnel engaged. Their total strength cannot be disclosed but it was much greater than any force previously used.

Up until this point in the war, several Commando raids had been carried out along the coast of occupied Europe, but all these operations combined did not see as many men deployed as had been at Dieppe.

The next part of the article was most probably the only bit that was incorrect, or was maybe more of an "official white lie", when it said that, 'From first to last, the operation went like clockwork.' As history has recorded, this was most definitely not the case.

> Before daylight very strong forces of fighters, accompanied by bombers, made a constant procession over the Channel. Heavy explosions from the Calais and Boulogne areas were followed by reverberations from further west.
>
> Shortly after eight o'clock a very big formation of fighters, coming from the direction of Dieppe,

swept low over the Southeast Coast, and were soon followed by others. Although early haze restricted visibility, the sound of machine and cannon gunfire from the Channel indicated that many dog-fights were in process.

As light and medium bombers supported the land operations, hundreds of fighters provided an air "umbrella" at all times. German fighters went up to engage them, and a Folkestone correspondent reported that Spitfires "seemed to fill the sky," while the roll of gunfire echoed across the channel with hardly a break.

At 10.30 am the Folkestone correspondent telephoned that the roll of guns from Northern France continued to echo across the Channel.

A large section of the article includes information about the air battle aspect of the raid. It describes how the Germans were believed to have a force of some 500-fighter aircraft based across northern France, which would cover the region of Dieppe: 'It is known that 82 of these were destroyed for certain, and that 100 more were probably destroyed or damaged.'

These losses, in just one day, was an outcome that Göring and his Luftwaffe could ill afford, not only in the number of aircraft lost, but also the number of experienced pilots as well. The article also included a particular interesting reference about the Soviet Union:

One indirect outcome of our air successes over Dieppe will probably be aid to Russia on the Eastern Front. This will be so if the Germans withdraw fighters from that front to replace their losses in the West.

The Germans have their greatest air strength lined up against the Soviet Union. Because of this, it may be from here that they will draw "reinforcements". But the Axis have air fleets elsewhere, in the Middle East and in the Balkans, for instance. And they need them in all these theatres. In any event, the Luftwaffe in the West have at least been made to fight. This had long been the aim of the R.A.F.

Thus, the Dieppe raid was an even greater contribution to the war situation as a whole, than appears on the surface.

Air protection unparalleled in our fighting history was provided for our ground forces. It was a very gratifying feature of the raid. Both the nation and the R.A.F. had been waiting for this day when our troops would get the air support they deserve.

On the same page as the reporting of the Dieppe Raid from a British perspective, another article describes the event from an American view point, which makes for interesting reading on how the war was being viewed in the United States.

America Electrified
Full Dress Rehearsal for the Second Front

New York, Wednesday – Some of the biggest headlines since Japan attacked Pearl Harbor and

America declared war appeared in today's evening papers, announcing that American troops had taken part in the Commando raid on Dieppe.

"We land in France" was the main headline of the *New York World Telegram*. The two biggest headlines, each six inches high, appeared in *The Sun* and the *Journal America*. *The Sun* had a three-line headline, "US troops land with Commandos in biggest raid". The *Journal America* had a two-line banner, "US and British invade France".

As the battle round Dieppe lasted well into the night here, many Americans began to ask themselves whether this might not after all, be the prelude to a real invasion despite the British denials.

This belief by some Americans could not have been a widely held one, as their military personnel had only begun arriving in the UK on 26 January 1942. The full-scale invasion of German-occupied Europe at Normandy began on 6 June 1944. The initial decision to undertake this operation had been made at the Trident Conference in Washington, where Churchill and Roosevelt discussed their future war strategy. Their meetings took place between 12 and 25 May 1943, more than a year earlier.
Returning to the article:

The presence of tanks and the constant shuttle of American, British and Canadian fighters and bombers from British bases, to provide the biggest aerial umbrella ever seen over the French coast, increased the belief that the United Nations forces were fully prepared, if some soft spot were found in the German defences, to press home and develop the attack, and establish a permanent bridgehead from which the United Nations forces could press forward toward the liberation of Europe.

The inclusion of US Rangers in the raid on Dieppe was viewed very positively by most sections of the American public, as well as leading politicians. Senator Reynolds, chairman of the Senate Military Affairs Committee, said:

The raid can be construed only as meaning that we are ready to open a Second Front. It is wonderful, the best news I have ever heard. Now we have the opportunity to show the world what this country can do in face-to-face combat. We will show the world that once American soldiers set foot on land, they cannot be budged.

Senator Reynolds' comments were a good example of just how excited the Americans were in their reaction to the raid on Dieppe. Out of the more than 6,000 Allied service men who had taken part in the raid, only fifty were American and even then they did not fight as a single unit. Instead, they were split in to small groups of no more than about four men and attached to British and Canadian units.

On the evening of the day of the raid, an American War Department spokesman said that it was possible the Dieppe Raid had been made with the dual purpose of making the Germans nervous and uncertain about the likelihood and location of future Allied raids, as well as providing British and American troops with experience in landing tanks and guns, even though it was fully understood that these may have to be subsequently abandoned.

It was noticeable that the American communique made absolutely no mention of the Canadian forces, who had provided the largest number of men for the raid and had also suffered the heaviest casualties.

The *Aberdeen Evening Express* newspaper of Wednesday, 9 September included an article concerning comments made by the German High Command about the raid on Dieppe:

Nazis' Dieppe Admissions

The first German admission as to the importance of the Dieppe raid was made today by a German broadcaster in a talk to North America in English.

He admitted that further raids must be expected, and that it would be possible for the British to establish themselves on the beaches for at least two days.

This clearly shows that the Germans realise that when we decide to make a landing with the intention of staying there for some time we can do so. It is the first time the Germans have admitted such a prospect, and until now the German propaganda machine has been insistent that it would be impossible for us to establish ourselves at any point on the Continent.

It would seem therefore that now the German General Staff have examined the implications of the Dieppe raid, they realise they are vulnerable.

The article is interesting in so far as its contents appear rather at odds with the reality of what actually took place. Why, after defeating an Allied raiding force of approximately 6,000 men in a raid which lasted somewhere in the region of just nine hours, with a ground force of just 1,500, would anybody on the German side make such comments? Dieppe was a catastrophic defeat for the Allies, which therefore means it was a propaganda victory for the Germans on a massive scale. The Germans also greatly benefitted from the experience and were thus able to improve on measures they already had in place to ensure that any similar Allied raid would be defeated even easier.

Only two sensible conclusions can be drawn from these comments: they were either made without any official approval, or it was simply an attempt at subterfuge on behalf of the Germans.

The *Nottingham Journal* of Thursday, 1 October included an article on its back page concerning the raid on Dieppe:

Premier Says Nearly Half of Dieppe Force Was Lost

Air support during the Dieppe raid was faultless, it was revealed by Mr Churchill yesterday.

He also disclosed that our losses were very heavy and went up to nearly half of the total force.

Mr Henderson Stewart (Ind.) asked the Prime Minister if he had been able to consider the full reports of the Service departments on the Dieppe raid, and in particular, upon the support afforded by the RAF to the Army; whether he was satisfied that the support was adequate and effective; and whether any further measures were to be taken to meet the demands of the Army for still closer support from the air arm in future actions?

Mr Churchill: During the course of the operation the military force commander made a signal which included the statement that air support was faultless. The answer to the second part is "Yes." As regards the third part, the problem of air support for the Army is under constant consideration.

No Inconsistency

Mr Henderson Stewart asked the Prime Minister if he would explain how the House should reconcile the announcement made on 8 September that most of the Dieppe invading force came back with the official statement of the Canadian Minister of National Defence that of 5,000 Canadian troops involved in the raid, casualties totalled 3,350 of whom 2,717 were killed or missing?

The Prime Minister replied: There is no inconsistency in this with the statement of the Canadian Minister of National Defence, who was referring only to casualties among the Canadian troops.

Mr Stokes (Lab): Are you able to make any general statement on the total losses in that raid?

Mr Churchill: I do not know that we need to be so meticulous as to give exact figures to the enemy.

Losses were very heavy and went up to nearly half of the total force.

This is a good example of the difficulties of wartime politics. Members of Parliament would, by the very nature of their position, ask difficult questions of any Prime Minister and his government. For Winston Churchill, it was a juggling act of keeping everybody within the House of Commons happy, which included his own MPs as well as those of opposition parties. It was only right and proper that he kept them, and the entire country, up to date with how the war was going, but he also had to be aware of not presenting finite details and information to enemy nations, which they in turn could then potentially use to their advantage and against British and Allied interests.

The total British and Canadian raiding force was somewhere in the region of 10,500 men and included the Canadian 2nd Infantry Division. British forces came from Nos. 3, 4, 10, 30, and 40 Commando, some 237 vessels from the Royal Navy and the 74 squadrons from the Royal Air Force. In addition, there were 50 men from the United States Army Rangers.

The Canadians lost 907 men, with a further 2,460 wounded. A total of 275 British Commandos were killed, along with 3 Americans. The Royal Navy suffered 550 men killed and wounded, whilst the Royal Air Force losses were 62 dead, 30 wounded with another 17 who were captured.

Approximately 2,000 Canadian soldiers were captured by the Germans at Dieppe, although initially it would not have been known by the Allies if these men had been killed or captured. As can be seen from the following article, the next of kin of all of these soldiers had to wait weeks to discover the fate of their loved ones. Initially they would have been informed by the Canadian authorities that their husbands, sons, brothers, fathers or uncles were "missing in action". Then it was simply a matter of sitting and waiting for confirmation as to what had happened, but until the German military authorities confirmed the names of those they had captured, the relatives could do little more.

The *Dundee Courier*, also dated Thursday, 1 October, provides a typical example of the plight of the POWs and relatives alike:

Captured in Dieppe Raid

Pte. Jerome Alvoet, of the Essex Scottish Regiment, Royal Canadian Army, previously reported missing in the Dieppe raid, is now reported a prisoner. Mrs Alvoet stays with her mother, Mrs. Thomas, 7 Hill Street, Dundee.

Private Jerome Gerard Alvoet had enlisted in the Canadian Army on 12 March 1940. Along with his comrades he left his native Canada on 17 July 1940, and arrived at Gourock, on the west coast of Scotland, on 2 August 1940.

His Army record shows that he 'embarked for France (Operation Jubilee)' on 18 August 1942, and that the following day he had been officially reported as 'Missing'. Just one day later, German military authorities informed their British counterparts that Alvoet had in fact been captured at Dieppe and had been allocated to Stalag IID, in Stargard, Poland.

After having been released from captivity after the camp was liberated by the Soviet Red Army in mid-April 1945, he was repatriated to the UK, where he arrived on 11 May 1945, and was sent immediately to the 4th Canadian General

Hospital to be given a comprehensive medical examination after having spent nearly three years in captivity as a POW. He spent six days at the hospital before he was discharged with a clean bill of health. From there he was sent to the 1st Canadian Reception Depot, but after being there for a month, at 23.59 hours on 16 June 1945, he went absent without leave and did not return until 13.15 on 10 July 1945. He was finally 'demobbed' from the Army on 12 February 1946 in London.

The *Buckingham Advertiser and Free Press* of Saturday, 17 October 1942, included the following article:

Chained Dieppe Prisoners
Mr David Wehl's Monthly Commentary

"The Chaining of the Dieppe Prisoners" was the subject of comment by Mr David Wehl (Ministry of Information Speaker) in his monthly War Commentary which he gave in Buckingham on Wednesday and Winslow on Monday. Mr Wehl observed that a great deal of nonsense had been written about this matter and went on to refer to the bombing, earlier in the war, by the bombing of lightships, pointing out that this and many other horrible deeds that they had committed, were against International Law and could have no definite war purpose.

We had been raiding the coasts of France, "pinching Germans" which, for very obvious reasons, we wanted alive, and this had been causing great annoyance to the enemy and there was no doubt that this retaliation on our prisoners was carried out in the hope of putting a stop to these raids. With regard to the treatment of prisoners it was quite correct to say that we had not broken any international rules whatever, because what went against all international law was to take reprisals on prisoners that they had already got. In his personal opinion, we were making a mistake in suggesting reprisals upon German prisoners, although it "might work".

It would be a terrible mistake if we both indulged in a long competition in the treatment of prisoners, because we did not know where it would end.

This story comes in part from the capture of Brigadier William Southam, the Commander-in-Chief of the Canadian 6th Infantry Brigade, who was himself captured at Dieppe. For some reason, maybe only known by himself, when he came ashore he had with him a copy of the Allied assault plan. On realising he was to be captured by the Germans, he attempted to bury the document on the beach, but his efforts were to no avail and it was soon discovered. The plan included the sentence, "wherever possible, prisoners' hands will be tied to prevent the destruction of their documents", which in the circumstances could not have been anymore ironic.

The discovery of the document went a long way to the issuing of Hitler's infamous Commando Order on 18 October 1942, which stated that all captured Allied Commandos in either the European or North African theatres of war should be treated as criminals and executed immediately without trial. This was regardless of whether they were in proper uniform or in the process of trying to surrender.

Although the discovery of Brigadier Southam's document may well have started the process which resulted in the issuing of Hitler's Commando Order, it certainly was not the only reason. What compounded matters even further was Operation Basalt, a raid carried out on the German-occupied Channel Island of Sark by just twelve men from No. 12 and No. 62 Commando of the Special Operations Executive's Small Scale Raiding Force, on the night of 3-4 October 1942. The purpose of the raid was reconnaissance and the capturing of a small number of German soldiers.

The small band of Commandos had left Portland at 19.00 on the evening of 3 October, arriving on the island later that evening. After having scaled the treacherous cliff face at a location known locally as the Hog's Back, the Commandos were led by Major Geoffrey Appleyard. Included in their number was the Dane Major Anders Lassen, who in 1945 was posthumously awarded the Victoria Cross, making him the only non-Commonwealth recipient of this award during the course of the Second World War.

The Commandos were informed by a local woman, Mrs Pittard, whose house they had broken into, that a number of German soldiers were billeted at an annex to the local Dixcart Hotel. After Major Lassen had despatched a German guard he discovered in a large hut at the front of the hotel, matters quickly started to get out of hand. The 'hut' contained six rooms where five other German soldiers were found asleep. The Commandos woke the surprised men. It was after they had taken them outside that the problems began. Rather than ending the raid with their five German prisoners, the Commandos decided to enter the hotel in an attempt to capture more prisoners. Consequently, to reduce the number of men they would have to leave behind to guard their newly acquired prisoners, they tied their hands with toggle ropes.

Whilst the main group of Commandos entered the hotel, the German prisoners outside had decided that they were not going to give up without a fight and started making a commotion in an attempt, no doubt, to wake up their colleagues in the hotel and let them know there was a problem. Whilst this was going on, three of the German prisoners tried to make a break for it. In the immediate aftermath one of them was shot dead, two more were shot and wounded, and another was stabbed.

Before matters got totally out of control and more Germans arrived at the scene, the Commandos escaped, roping their way down the cliff face, recovering their concealed boat and making their way back across the English Channel to the safety of their base at Portland. They had managed to do all this without losing a single man, and had brought back with them one German prisoner by the name of Hermann Weinrich.

Adolf Hitler was informed of the raid and that some of his men had been captured and had their hands tied, while three of them had been shot. It is unclear as to whether he had been provided with the complete picture, but on 9 October 1942, he ordered that 1,376 Allied POWs held in German custody, many of whom were Canadians captured at Dieppe, should be shackled. This action was in turn reciprocated on German POWs held in Canada.

Although an abstract failure for the Allies, lessons were most definitely learned from the raid on Sark, which undoubtedly helped in future raids as well as the eventual D-Day landings in June 1944. The Dieppe Raid showed the need for the element of surprise, up-to-date intelligence on enemy defensive positions, aerial bombardments of such positions, avoidance of frontal assaults on heavily defended port areas, and purpose-built landing craft. Although this was the reality, the Press put a slightly different slant on events. By way of example, one newspaper, *The Coventry Evening Post*, carried the following headline on 8 September 1942: 'Dieppe Raid Prelude To Full Scale Operations', with a following sub-heading of, 'Enemy Does Not Know Where And When We Will Strike'.

In response to the raid, Prime Minister Winston Churchill informed the House of Commons: 'The Dieppe Raid was a hard, savage clash, such as are likely to become increasingly numerous as the war deepens. We had to get the information necessary before launching operations on a much larger scale.'

There was not one word, either in the Press or from the lips of Winston Churchill about the raid having been a resounding defeat for the Allies. Neither was there any mention of the extent of casualties and the number of those captured.

CHAPTER THIRTEEN

The Enigma Pinch

As has already been discussed elsewhere in this book, there have been a number of suggestions as to why the raid on Dieppe took place, but what is fact and what is fiction can sometimes be hard to determine.

Research carried out by the Canadian historian David O'Keefe has suggested that during the Dieppe Raid, what was known as a "pinch operation" took place in an effort to locate and capture a much sought-after, new style German Enigma cipher machine, along with its related code books used for sending encrypted military communications.

Enigma machines were used extensively by the German military during the course of the Second World War to send top secret messages in the misbelief that it was totally secure, which of course it was not. The Enigma Key had been broken for operations on the Eastern Front on 9 July 1942 by British cryptologists at Bletchley Park, but British and Polish cryptologists had already broken a number of the Enigma codes for the Western Front before that.

The machine worked on an electromechanical rotor mechanism and for messages to be successfully received, the receiving station had to be aware of the settings the sending station had used to send the message in the first place. If they were not in possession of this information, they would not be able to decode and make sense of the message successfully. To make matters even more difficult for the code breakers, the settings used were usually changed every day.

Britain's war time code-breaking headquarters was situated at Bletchley Park in Buckinghamshire. The building and the 58 acres it rests in were purchased in May 1938 by Admiral Sir Hugh Sinclair, who at the time was in charge of the Secret Intelligence Service, later MI6, specifically for use by the Government Code and Cypher School and the Secret Intelligence Service in the event of the outbreak of war. Just over a year later, Sir Hugh's concerns became an unwanted reality.

During the Second World War, Bletchley was a hive of activity where mathematicians and scientists spent their time intercepting German radio transmissions and trying to break German secret codes to allow them to be in possession of much needed, top secret enemy information. It has been estimated that the work undertaken at Bletchley Park shortened the war by up to two years.

During the early years of the war, Britain relied heavily for food stuffs and military hardware on imports from the United States. This meant keeping the Allied shipping which used the waters of the Atlantic Ocean safe from German U-boat attacks. This was imperative to Britain staying in the war. A lot of the work undertaken at Bletchley Park went a long way to ensuring that more of the shipping that made its way across the Atlantic to British ports completed their journeys safely.

Unbeknown to the Germans, the boffins at Bletchley Park had broken the secret of the Enigma machine back in

July 1941, but in February 1942, this relatively short-lived advantage was lost when the German Navy replaced their three-rota machines with the new M4 version, which had a four-rotor system, for use by their submarines. Hence why the need to capture one of these new machines was of the utmost urgency.

It is claimed that the troops who were specifically deployed to capture the Enigma machine at Dieppe were from No. 30 Commando, or the 30 Assault Unit. Although men from that particular unit are known to have taken part in the raid, it was not officially formed until September 1942, the month after the raid on Dieppe took place. It is, of course, more than possible that they were already in place before that date. After all, this was a time of war, where not everything was always as it might at first appear to be.

This new unit was made up of four troops: 33 (Royal Marines), 34 (Army), 35 (Royal Air Force), and 36 (Royal Navy). Their main purpose was to gather intelligence, of whatever kind, by means of covert operations from behind enemy lines. Because of the varied make-up of men in the unit, it was able to carry out any such infiltrations by land, sea or air, making it an extremely useful resource. One of the unit's senior officers was Commander Ian Fleming, the man who went on to become the well-known post-war author behind the James Bond novels. Fleming worked under Admiral John Godfrey, who was the head of Britain's Naval Intelligence.

From a historical perspective, the 30 Assault Unit took part in the raid as No. 40 Royal Marine Commando.

There is every possibility that Fleming's Commandos had been tasked with recovering an Enigma set, but it is impossible to believe that this was the sole reason why the raid on Dieppe took place. It is more likely that British Naval Intelligence seized an opportunity to be part of an operation which had already been planned so that they could try to obtain one of the new Enigma machines.

As with the overall plan for the raid on Dieppe having been undermined by poor intelligence, the information which British Naval Intelligence had about an Enigma machine being located at Dieppe was not exactly what could be called watertight. It was known that the German naval headquarters at Dieppe were at the Hotel Moderne, located close to the town's seafront, and this was consequently No. 40 Royal Marine Commando's main target at Dieppe. However, whether the Germans actually had any Enigma machines at the Hotel Moderne was nothing more than guess work, but it was a guess that, if right, could have helped to change the course of the war.

Whatever the truth about whether the raid on Dieppe was purely to try to capture an Enigma machine, most of the men tasked with stealing it never actually made it ashore. The officers and men of No. 40 Commando had made their way to Dieppe on board the flat-bottomed, 197-foot-long Dragonfly-class gunboat HMS *Locust*, arriving off Dieppe at about 05.30, before transferring into a number of landing craft to make their way to the beaches east of the main harbour. However, having sustained intense machine gun and mortar fire as they made their final approach, the Commandos' commanding officer, Lieutenant Colonel J.P. Phillips, gave the order to abort the landings and make their way back out to sea. In the caotic confusion of battle, the second-in-command, Major General Robert Dyer "Titch" Houghton, did not receive the order, and instead continued onto the beach. Along with a number of his men, he was subsequently captured at Dieppe and spent the rest of the war as a POW. Out of 370 officers and men of No. 40 Commando involved in the raid, 76 were killed, including Lieutenant Colonel Philips.

Later in the war, members of the 30 Assault Unit, possibly including some of those who took part in the raid at Dieppe, landed on Juno Beach on 6 June 1944, along with Canadian forces, as part of the Normandy D-Day landings. Their specific task was to capture a German radar station at Douvres-la-Délivrande, just north of Caen. The battle for this location took place on 17 June 1944. Some accounts of this raid refer to the men of 30 Assault Unit as being part of No. 41 Commando, Royal Marines.

It is known that as part of the raid on Dieppe, HMS *Locust* was deployed to seize several landing barges and trawlers moored in the town's harbour and tow them back to England. There were somewhere in the region of 200 Royal Marine Commandos on board, which included those from the 30 Assault Unit. This would appear to be a large number of men just to help tow some vessels back to England. Despite numerous attempts, HMS *Locust* never made it into Dieppe harbour, and the Royal Marines on board never made it ashore, no matter what the truth is about the real purpose of their mission.

Even though no Enigma machine of any kind was discovered during the raid, there was an urgent need on the part of the Allies to gain possession of one. If the transmissions sent via these machines could not be decoded, and quickly, the consequences in loss of life, food, and military equipment, could have been devastating for the Allies.

CHAPTER FOURTEEN

1er Bataillon de Fusiliers Marins Commandos

Fifteen men from the French Fusiliers Marins took part in the raid on Dieppe. This elite unit was made up of men from the Free French Navy, and the man in charge was the formidable and charismatic Lieutenant de Vaisseau (Captain) Philippe Kieffer, MBE, MC, a hero of the Free French Forces.

Born in Haiti to an English mother, Kieffer was educated in Chicago, USA, before working for a bank in New York City. Already 40 by the outbreak of the Second World War, this did not deter him from becoming directly involved. As an officer in the French Navy Reserve, he enlisted in the French Navy and was involved in the Battle of Dunkirk in May - June 1940, before arriving in London on 19 June.

Kieffer was one of the very first to join the Forces Navales Francaises Libres (Free French Naval Forces) on the very day it was formed, 1 July 1940, a month after the British Commandos had been formed. Having become aware of their existence and impressed with their training and the roles they were expected to carry out, in May 1941 he approached

Admiral Émile Henry Muselier, commander of the Free French Naval Forces, and requested that he be allowed to set up his own Commando unit. Muselier gave his approval and Kieffer founded the 1re Compagnie de Fusiliers-Marins (1st Company of Naval Rifles), a unit of some forty men.

The 1er Bataillon de Fusiliers Marins Commandos was a Commando unit formed in May 1942. When Troop 1 of the battalion was formed, the original intention was to make its strength some 400 officers and men in preparation for the expected Allied offensive operations throughout Europe. Initially, the unit had its headquarteres in the Portsmouth area on the south coast of England whilst undergoing basic training, before it headed off to Scotland to undergo training at the Commando Training Centre at Achnacarry.

Situated as it was some 15 miles north of Fort William, Achnacarry was an ideal location for a Commando training base and would see approximately 25,000 men complete their training there during the Second World War. The training itself was both brutal and realistic, including live firing exercises, which resulted in a number of recruits being wounded and killed.

Although keeping their own identity, Kieffer's men became part of No. 10 (Inter-Allied) Commando, a unit of the British Army but whose members were non-British, coming from a number of European countries such as France, the Netherlands, Belgium, Norway, Poland, Denmark and Yugoslavia, all of which were occupied by German forces.

Fifteen of Kieffer's men from No. 1 (French) Troop, No. 10 (Inter-Allied) Commando, took part in the raid on Dieppe whilst attached to No. 3 and No. 4 Commando, along with the Canadian forces, but whilst wearing their Free French Forces insignia and headgear. Their main purpose was to act as interpreters between the Allied forces, French civilians and/or members of the local resistance movement. They were also tasked with collecting and gathering any useful intelligence information, and, if possible, were to try to persuade any young Frenchmen of a fighting age to return with them to England and enlist in the Free French Forces.

Those members of the unit who landed with Lovat's No. 4 Commando on Orange Beach faired best, with their overall target being the artillery battery at Varengeville, which turned out to be the most successful part of the raid. Those members attached to No. 3 Commando, led by Lieutenant Colonel John Durnford-Slater, were tasked with landing on Yellow Beach to take out the artillery battery, referred to by the Allies as Goebbels, located to the west of the town near Berneval. These men faired a lot worse as on their way onto the beach, they unexpectedly encountered a number of German S-boats escorting an oil tanker. The S-boats opened fire on the surprised Commandos, and a number of them never made it to the beach, let alone to their intended target. In total only eighteen men from No. 3 Commando made it ashore, which meant that taking out the defensive battery, and thus preventing its seven guns from firing on the main landings, was always going to be difficult to achieve.

The main assault of the raid took place in the centre of Dieppe on what had been designated as Red and White beaches, and involved units from the Essex Scottish Regiment and the Royal Hamilton Light Infantry. Due to the lack of intended support of Churchill tanks from the 14th Army Tank Regiment, the two attacking units quickly began to sustain heavy casualties. The decision was then taken by the Canadian commander, Major General Roberts, to send in two of his reserve units, one of which was the Fusiliers Mont-Royal, under the command of Lieutenant Colonel Dollard Ménard. As the twenty-six landing craft sailed towards their beach, the men were heavily engaged by the Germans, who hit them with heavy machine gun, mortar and grenade fire, destroying a number of the landing craft in the process. The result of this was that only a few men made it to the beach, and those who did were soon pinned down under the cliffs, where they remained until they were either captured or killed.

It has only been possible to establish minimum details of the Free French Forces who took part in the raid, for most this has simply been their rank and surname. Where further information has been discovered about a specific individual, this has been included.

Attached to No. 4 Commando

Sergeant François Baloche (awarded the Military Medal for his gallant and distinguished actions)
Corporal Taverne
Fusilier R. Rabouhans

Attached to Canadian Forces

Lieutenant Guy Vourc'h
Sergeant Raymond Dumenoir
Private Loverini
Private Simon
Private Jean
Private Borettini
Private Tanniou

Attached to No. 3 Commando

Sergeant De Wandelaer
Sergeant Moutaillier
Corporal Cesar
Corporal Ropert
Corporal Errard

Of the Frenchmen who took part in the raid, three of them, Lieutenant Guy Vourc'h, Private Louis Serge Moutaillier and Corporal Cesar, were captured. Cesar eventually escaped from captivity and made his way back to England, whilst Moutaillier was not so fortunate. There are two versions concerning his death. Firstly, that he was captured at Dieppe and once it had been discovered he was a Commando, he was executed under Hitler's Commando Order, which deemed that all such captured combatants be shot. The other version is that he was killed in action at Dieppe, having initially been reported as being missing presumed dead.

Marine Nationale Naval Forces in the UK confirmed in a letter addressed to the head of the Central Service of the Etat Civil (Register of Births, Marriages and Deaths) in Paris, dated 24 May 1945, that Moutailleur had disappeared during the raid on Dieppe, and no news had been received about him since.

CHAPTER FIFTEEN

Canadian Military Report No. 83 – 19 September 1942

Between 1940 and 1948, Canadian Military Headquarters issued a number of reports chronicling Canadian actions during the Second World War. They were researched and compiled by Canadian Army military personnel, which in the main meant just one man, Major (later Colonel) Charles Perry Stacey. Stacey was well known for his attention to detail and leaving no stone unturned in his research. Having begun his military career with the Canadian Corps of Signals in 1924, he was able to combine his military service whilst continuing his education, receiving a BA in History from the University of Toronto in 1924, a second BA in History in 1929 whilst a student at Oxford University, and a doctorate from Princeton University in 1933. Unsurprisingly, he would then go on to teach history at Princeton from 1933 to 1940.

A number of these reports issued by the Canadian Military Headquarters concerned different aspects of the raid on Dieppe, three of which are included within the pages of this book. The main reason for including these specific reports is to try to provide some balance and clarity in relation to certain comments and observations about the raid that were made by members of staff from the office of Combined Operations, or attempts by them to leave out certain points or claims which portrayed the raid in a negative manner from the initial reports.

In an attempt to put a positive spin on the raid, Allied commanders claimed that valuable military information was gained, while Admiral Lord Mountbatten made the claim that 'for every soldier who died at Dieppe, ten were saved on D-Day'. That is an easy statement to make, but extremely difficult to evidence. It has been difficult for historians to fully challenge and evaluate the part played by Combined Operations as there were no written records of the planning, or of the approval given by the Chiefs of Staff for the raid to go ahead. Maybe this was intentional. It is possible that Mountbatten went ahead with the operation without authorisation to do so. This leaves Combined Operations open to the suggestion that the operation failed because those involved in its planning were restricted by a lack of strategic skills at the highest level. In support of this suggestion comes the fact that the Operation Order for Jubilee was extremely detailed, consisting of 121 typewritten pages. This is not an aspect of the raid that any of the planners wanted to highlight.

The three reports to be examined here are as follows:

No. 83. – Preliminary Report on Operation "Jubilee": The Raid on Dieppe, 19 Aug '42 (19 September 1942)

No. 100. – Operation "Jubilee": The Raid on Dieppe, 19 Aug '42. Part 1: The Preliminaries of the Operation (16 July 1943)

No. 142. – Operation "Jubilee": The Raid on Dieppe, 19 Aug '42. Further New Information (18 July 1945)

A number of other Canadian reports were issued in connection with the raid, but not all of them can be included in this book. However, should the reader wish to find out more, they include the following:

No. 89. – The Operation at Dieppe, 19 Aug '42: Personal Stories of Participants (31 December 1942)

No. 90. – The Operation at Dieppe, 19 Aug '42: Further Personal Stories of Participants (18 February 1943)

No. 98. – Article Dealing with the Operation at Dieppe, 19 Aug '42 (15 July 1943)

No. 101. – Operation "Jubilee": The Raid on Dieppe, 19 Aug '42 (11 August 1943)

No. 107. – The Operation at Dieppe, 19 Aug '42: Further Personal Stories of Participants (29 November 1943)

No. 108. – Operation "Jubilee": The Raid on Dieppe, 19 Aug '42. Part II: The Execution of the Operation. Section 2: The Attack on the Main Beaches (17 December 1943)

No. 109. – Operation "Jubilee": The Raid on Dieppe, 19 Aug '42. Part III: Some Special Aspects

No. 116. – Operation "Jubilee": The Raid on Dieppe, 19 Aug '42. Additional information from German Sources (10 May 1944)

No. 128. – The Operation at Dieppe, 19 Aug '42. Some New Information (20 November 1944)

No. 130. – The Operation at Dieppe, 19 Aug '42: Pictorial and Cartographical Material (27 November 1944)

No. 153. – Operation "Jubilee": The Raid on Dieppe, 19 Aug '42. New Light on planning (22 March 1946)

No. 159. – Operation "Jubilee": The Raid on Dieppe, 19 Aug '42, Additional Information on Planning (5 October 1946)

Report No. 83, dated 19 September 1942, is thirteen pages long and had originally been marked as SECRET, before eventually being declassified on 7 August 1988.

The report's first paragraph include a reference to Appendix A, which in essence was a draft, originally prepared with a view to it being published by the Canadian government.

The report was split into two. The first two pages feature Major Stacey's brief overview of the experience and history of Canadian forces in the UK up to the time of the raid. It includes the numbers of Canadian forces who took part in it, those who returned, and the difficulties he had experienced in preparing a report that was acceptable to senior Canadian and British military personnel involved in the planning of the raid, and the Canadian government.

The second part of the report is what is referred to as Appendix A. When going through the first part of Stacey's report, paragraph three includes the following:

> This was an extremely hazardous operation involving an attack on a very strong position (the strength of which, moreover, is now admitted to have been somewhat underestimated) and our losses were very heavy. A preliminary report indicates that the total number of Canadian troops embarked for the operation was 4,912 (304 officers, 4,608 other ranks). There returned a total of 2,147 (109 officers, 2,038 other ranks). These figures are to be regarded as merely approximate; in a subsequent report it is hoped to provide final ones.
>
> On 15 Sep '42 the Canadian Government announced that the total Canadian casualties in the operation amounted to 3,350 dead, wounded and missing (*Times*, London, 16 Sep '42). The heaviest losses were suffered by 4 Cdn Inf Bde, which embarked 94 officers and 1,604 other ranks, and brought back 17 officers and 334 other ranks.

It is interesting to note that the first few lines of the report refer to the fact that not only was Dieppe heavily defended, but the belief of just how many Germans were there had been underestimated, which could be interpreted to mean that the Canadian's sustained many more casualties than had been expected.

As the Germans had managed to capture a copy of the Allied Operational Order for the raid, the Canadian government felt that it would be possible to put together a detailed report, in the form of a "White Paper" about the operation, for the consumption of the Canadian public. But before the final content of the report could be agreed, it first appeared in a draft format. Point 5 of this report contained the following:

> When, however, this draft was subsequently submitted to Combined Operations Headquarters, the authorities there took exception to many passages in it. It then appeared that C.O.H.Q. strongly objected to, among other things, the publication of any material which might seem, even by implication, to admit the loss of the Operational Order. The Chief of the Combined Operations (Vice-Admiral Lord Louis MOUNTBATTEN) told Brigadier YOUNG (then B.G.S., C.M.H.Q.) that the publication of this draft would be worth £500,000 to the enemy. Accordingly, the draft was revised by the Public Relations staff of C.O.H.Q. (the actual work being done, curiously enough, by a United States officer, Major Lawrence, who is a member of that staff). The writer then again revised his account, following the general lines of Major LAWRENCE'S draft, but using as far as possible, under instructions from C.M.H.Q., the words of his own original version.

The report by Major Stacey was written in a numbered paragraph format, with his draft owing much to the preliminary report about the raid, as written by General Roberts. Another section came from his own notes, written down on 27 August 1942, concerning remarks made by General McNaughton to a group of visiting Canadian newspaper editors during an interview he gave at Headley Court, near Leatherhead, the Canadian forces' European headquarters at the time.

To ensure that the operation provided Canadian military planners with as much operational intelligence as was possible, it was directed that all Canadian forces who returned from the raid were to make detailed written statements about their individual experiences. Copies of these personal accounts were subsequently attached as appendices to the War Diaries of the regiments to which these men belonged.

The second part of the document, Appendix A, which is what Major Stacey referred to at the beginning of his report, began with the following paragraph:

> It is now possible to give fuller details of the Combined Operation against the enemy forces in the Dieppe area, carried out on 19 August by forces which included a large body of the Canadian Army Overseas. This account is based upon the preliminary report made by the Military Force Commander (Major-General J.H. Roberts, M.C., G.O.C. 2nd Canadian Division) and upon examination of personal reports made by many participants including a large number of N.C.Os. and private soldiers, and statements by enemy prisoners of war.

This part of the report covers different aspects of the raid on Dieppe and is broken down into the following five sub-headings.

Objects and Preliminaries of the Operation

This highlighted two reasons for the raid taking place. It started off by talking about how it was hoped that such operations would help ensure that Germany had to deploy and maintain large numbers of her forces in Western Europe, which by doing so would prevent their deployment elsewhere in other theatres of war, such as Russia. Secondly, it was believed that the raid would provide those who took part in it with invaluable experience which could then be utilised at a later date in similar operations.

The local objectives for the raid were defined in the Operational Order for Jubilee:

> Operation Jubilee is a raid on Dieppe with limited military and air objectives, embracing the destruction of local defences, power stations, harbour installations, rolling stock, etc., in Jubilee, the capture of prisoners, the destruction of an aerodrome near the town and the capture and removal of German invasion barges and other craft in the harbour.

It is quite clear from the outset of reading this second part of Major Stacey's report what he meant when he discussed earlier how senior military officers from the Combined Operations Headquarters had taken exception to some of the content of his original draft report concerning the raid on Dieppe.

One of the statements included in the final report that was known to be incorrect was that, 'This operation was most carefully prepared in advance in every detail'. If that was the case, why were Canadian forces deployed to conduct a full-frontal assault on the harbour area, knowing full well that it would be heavily defended, thus making it an objective extremely difficult to achieve?

The exact strength and location of all the German defences was not known to the planners, and the make-up of the beach being of large pebbles, rather than sand, and thus making it hard for landing tanks to gain any purchase on, appears to have been missed altogether.

The more the claims are made that everything possible was done to check and re-check the relevant facts about the preparations for the raid, the more preposterous they appear, as can be seen in the following paragraph:

> The officers charged with planning the operation had at their disposal a great mass of information relating to the Dieppe area collected from many sources. The proposed operation was checked on a large-scale model of the area to be raided, and when the plans were complete a most thorough understanding had been established between the three services.

The more the report has been changed to meet with the approval of the senior officers at Combined Operations Headquarters, the more laughable it becomes. It is already known that the two full-scale exercises which took place as part of the preparation for the raid on Dieppe were Yukon I and Yukon II. What is also known is that Lieutenant General Montgomery was so unimpressed with what he saw during that first exercise, including troops being landed on the wrong beaches and the tank landing craft arriving more than an hour late, he ordered it to be undertaken again, hence Exercise Yukon II. Compare these known facts with the following paragraph of the report:

> In the first instance the plans as developed were tried out in a full-scale exercise in which the whole force landed on a section of the coast and established a temporary bridgehead in the manner proposed for

the actual operation. Subsequently the results of this exercise were carefully analyzed and the plans modified accordingly. Another full-scale exercise then took place and the arrangements as modified were found to be much more satisfactory than before. After further analysis and consideration it was decided that the operation might now proceed.

There is no mention whatsoever here about Montgomery's displeasure at what he had observed during Exercise Yukon I.

The report's next paragraph discussed what in essence was Operation Rutter and covers the reasons why it was postponed. It makes no mention of the fact that Montgomery strongly recommended the entire operation should be cancelled, as all the men taking part in the raid had been briefed about the operation, and it would therefore be extremely difficult to keep its existence a secret. It also makes no mention of the fact that the reason the raid subsequently went ahead, under the name of Operation Jubilee, was because of the insistence of Vice Admiral Lord Louis Mountbatten.

The Course of the Operation

This section of the report includes information about the separate landing points of the raiding party and how successful each of them were in achieving their objectives. In relation to No. 3 Commando, who were under the overall command of Lieutenant Colonel Durnford-Slater, landed at Berneval, or to give its official coding for the raid, Yellow Beach, the report highlights the fact that whilst making their way towards the beach, at 03.00 the group came into contact with a number of German naval vessels escorting a tanker. This quite clearly forewarned the German defenders at Berneval, who from that point in time would have been on high alert. Here is a statement from the report about this aspect of the raid:

> Due to these circumstances only a small proportion of the Commando force intended for this duty, succeeded in landing, although too few to attack the enemy battery, sniped at the gunners throughout the operation, and to a certain extent succeeded in interfering with their fire.

Noticeably, it made no mention of the fact that the German naval vessels No. 3 Commando had come into contact with had been picked up by British radar stations along the south coast of England at 20.30 the previous evening, and that this same information was not passed on to the Commandos. The report also makes no mention of the fact that a number of the landing craft were lost in the encounter with the German vessels.

Yellow Beach was split into two areas: Yellow One, where six landing craft led by Captain R.L. Willis and consisting of around 119 men, came ashore; and Yellow Two, where just one landing craft, under the command of Captain Peter Young, with twenty men on board hit the beach.

The report also makes no mention of the breakdown in communications between the landing craft on the way into the beach. There was also no mention of the fact that only 1 of the 119 men who landed on Yellow One escaped and made it back to England, with 37 others being killed and the remaining 81 captured.

In relation to the Cameron Highlanders, who landed on Green Beach alongside the South Saskatchewan Regiment, the report said of them: 'During their advance they inflicted considerable losses on the enemy. They had not reached their objective, when they received the order to withdraw.'

The reality of their situation was somewhat different. They did not reach their objective because they were forced back by German reinforcements and sustained numerous casualties as they made their way back towards the beach. The Commonwealth War Graves Commission records the details of sixty-five members of the Queen's Own Cameron Highlanders of Canada as being killed at Dieppe on 19 August, but does not include the details of those who were wounded and subsequently died of their wounds.

In relation to the Churchill tanks that landed at Dieppe, the report said the following:

> Despite the fact that a number of these were soon immobilised by damage, their crews continued to fire their guns with the greatest of courage, engaging the batteries which were firing on the landing craft, and on the evidence of witnesses, contributed to the safe withdrawal of the latter.

What the report conveniently did not mention is that not one member of the tank crews managed to escape, with all of them either being killed or captured.

The next part of the report is quite shocking as it describes a complete contradiction of the facts:

> About one hour after the first landing at this point, information was received indicating that the beach was sufficiently cleared to permit the landing of the floating reserve. In consequence the Fusiliers

> Mont-Royal, commanded by Lt-Col. D. Menard, were ordered to land, and establish themselves on the beach and on the edge of the town of Dieppe.

Major General Roberts, who was unaware of what the situation was on the beaches and in the town due to a combination of a lack of radio communications and a heavy smoke screen that still covered the beaches, sent in his reserve units. These consisted of men from No. 40 Commando, Royal Marines, who the report made absolutely no mention of whatsoever, and Fusiliers Mont-Royal. Most of the twenty-six landing craft containing the Fusiliers never made it, having come under attack from German heavy machine gun fire, along with mortars and grenades. Only a small number of these men made it ashore, across the beach and into the town. The Commonwealth War Graves list 109 of them of these men as being killed during the raid. It was a similar fate for the Royal Marines, with most of them not making it ashore, while for nearly all of those who did, their fate was to be either captured or killed. The same records also list twenty-two members of No. 40 Commando as being killed at Dieppe.

Naval and Air Support

The report spoke in the highest possible terms of the support provided by both the Royal Navy and the Royal Air Force:

> The splendid assistance given by the Royal Navy has already been referred to. Throughout, it was beyond praise, and there are file statements by many members of the Canadian military forces, from private soldiers upwards, which testify to their

deep understanding and appreciation of the manner in which the Naval forces ran all risks to assist the troops.

Air Cover and bombing were likewise magnificent and drew similar warm tributes from the troops and from the Navy. Throughout the operation, both the Air Force and the Navy provided smoke screens which were highly effective, except in the area closest to shore (where a slight offshore breeze appears to have interfered) and which greatly reduced casualties to ships and personnel.

The effectiveness of the air support provided by the Allied aircraft who took part in the raid, is not open to question, and rightly deserves the positive comments and platitudes they received. After all, in an effort to ensure the Luftwaffe were unable to freely attack the Allied landings and the subsequent evacuation, 2,500 sorties were flown and 100 Allied aircraft lost, resulting in the deaths of sixty-two pilots and other crew members. A further thirty were wounded, while seventeen were captured and became POWs. The good work carried out by the RAF was hampered to some degree because with the deployed aircraft operating far from their home bases back in England, a number of aircraft, Spitfires in particular, were at the limit of their flying range. This meant that in some cases they could spend no longer than five minutes in the skies over Dieppe. There was, of course, absolutely no mention of this in the report.

The designated war room for intelligence and communications, based at the 11 Group Headquarters back in England, did not work anywhere as effectively as had been planned for. In fact, it quickly became overwhelmed due to the volume of messages being received as the number of Luftwaffe aircraft that became involved in the air battle over Dieppe increased. This resulted in vital messages not being passed on and led to some of the arriving German reinforcement formations being missed.

Results of the Operation

This part of the report consisted of six paragraphs, three of which particularly attract attention. The third paragraph states the following:

> One thing, however, can be stated with complete confidence. The organisation of combined command worked out in such detail in advance of the operation functioned perfectly. In particular, the method of organising the close support effort of the fighter cover provided by the R.A.F., a new method of control here employed for the first time, proved to be most satisfactory. The three services worked together in perfect co-operation, and in this respect the result of the operation has been to afford complete confidence in the effective co-ordination of the efforts of the three services in Combined Operations.

As was highlighted earlier in this chapter, there was no mention of the system in place in the War Room at II Group Headquarters at Uxbridge in Middlesex being inadequate to cope with the information it was expected to have to deal with.

Nor was there any mention that most of the fighter aircraft sent across the English Channel to take part in the raid used up so much fuel travelling there and back that many of them were only able to remain in the skies over Dieppe for a very short period of time.

The fifth paragraph, meanwhile, goes on to say:

> The forces engaged, and particularly the land forces, paid a very heavy price. The history of similar operations in the past serves to indicate that heavy losses are to be expected in amphibious operations of this type directed against a fortified coastline held by a determined and alert enemy. The landing operations in Gallipoli in the last war are a case in point.

This can arguably be seen as one of the most staggeringly incompetent comments included in a wartime report. Despite knowing the inherent dangers, and the likely outcome of deploying such a tactic, the Combined Operations hierarchy still went ahead and did it. If that was not bad enough, they then give the landings at Gallipoli in February 1915 as an example, meaning that the senior officers running the operation had twenty-seven years to improve upon the carnage of that failed operation. But in essence all they had apparently learned was how to make the exact same mistake again.

The last paragraph covers the Canadian part in the raid and how their troops had gained valuable combat experience which would put them in good stead for future wartime operations they might become involved in. It also says that those who returned were keen for another opportunity to fight the Germans so as to exact a revenge for the number of their comrades who were lost at Dieppe. It does not include anything on how they may also have been left feeling extremely frustrated and angry following so many of their comrades being killed, in what must have been seen by them to have been a poorly organised operation. It does, however, say that, 'The Canadian units engaged in the Dieppe operation gained combat experience which will be of great value to them in future operations'.

There was no explanation as to why or how such a poorly planned and executed operation, which resulted in so many Allied casualties, would prove to be of great value to those who survived any future operations which they subsequently took part in.

The following appears to have been written purely for the purposes of keeping up the moral of the Canadian public:

> The troops have returned from the operation with added confidence in themselves and, in particular, in the leadership of their officers and N.C.O.s, which throughout the operation was of the very highest order.

> All ranks of the units concerned, and especially those which suffered most heavily, are anxious for another opportunity of contact with the enemy which will enable them to exact from him a further reckoning for the losses which they have suffered on this occasion.

In the first sentence the use of the words 'added confidence' seem slightly out of place. Those Canadian soldiers who survived the debacle and returned to England would more likely have been somewhat shell-shocked, frustrated, and angry at what they had experienced. The second sentence follows a similar theme of confusing descriptions, such as explaining how the survivors of the raid, 'are anxious for another opportunity of contact with the enemy,' so they may take their revenge on the Germans. In the circumstances, it is more than likely that the survivors who returned to England after the raid were more concerned that the next time they saw action, it would be a repeat of what had happened to them at Dieppe.

Nevertheless, the final sentence of the report is possibly one of the only ones that is reported correctly: 'The heroism both of those who fell and those who returned will be a source of future inspiration to all ranks of the Canadian Army.'

There is no mention of the hundreds who had been captured and would spend three years of their lives incarcerated in a German POW camp thanks to such a poorly planned operation, or the utter frustration and anger of those who returned following the loss of so many of their comrades.

What was learned from the raid on Dieppe? The answer to that question could best be described in one single statement: that it was the best possible example of how not to undertake an amphibious landing.

CHAPTER SIXTEEN

Canadian Military Report No. 100 – 16 July 1943

Report No. 100, which is dated 16 July 1943, was originally classified as SECRET and was not officially declassified until 7 August 1986. It covers the planning and preliminaries of the operation.

One of the first points of interest about this report is the fact that in the planning for Operation Rutter, the town of Quiberville, some 12 miles west of Dieppe, had been discussed as a potential landing site for the raid. The man who came up with the initial idea for landings to take place here was Canadian Army officer Lieutenant Colonel Churchill C. Mann. The idea was dismissed because river obstacles could well have affected the successful landing of tanks. It was believed that tanks landing at Quiberville might just be able to seize the airfield at St Aubin, along with the high ground south of Dieppe. The downside of landing tanks there was that for them to make their way to Dieppe, they would need to cross two rivers: the Saâne and the Scie, meaning that arrangements would need to be made to seize the bridges which cross them to prevent the Germans from demolishing the structures themselves.

Planning for the raid had begun in early April 1942 and was carried out by the Target Committee of Combined Operations Headquarters shortly after the more successful raid at St Nazaire on 28 March 1942.

Nevertheless, how Dieppe was then subsequently chosen as the main landing site is a mystery. The report included the following comments: 'The coast in the Dieppe area consists in the main of steep cliffs generally unscalable by landing parties. Immediately to the west of the town these reach a height of 91 metres, and there is a similar, though less lofty headland to the east.'

Just as concerning was the following:

> The beach itself is composed of large "shingle", the stones being in some cases about the size of a man's fist. It is rough and irregular in contour. The slope, it appears, varies from about 1:7 to 1:4. (See the report by Major B. Sucharov, R.C.E., dated 2 Sep 42.)

> The forgoing description of the area will make it clear that the Dieppe region offered important natural obstacles to an attack from the sea. During their occupation of the town from June 1940, down to the time of the attack in August 1942, the Germans had constructed artificial defences which, supplementing these natural advantages, had the effect of rendering Dieppe a decidedly strong place.

The obvious question here is if Stacey was able to discover this information by July 1943, were those same facts known a year earlier, when Dieppe was being planned?

Once Dieppe had been chosen as the main landing point for the Allied troops and their tanks, Mann wrote the following:

> Such a plan, on the face of it, is almost a fantastic conception of the place most suited to a strong force of A.F.V. (Tanks). It is, however, well worth evaluating with an unbiased mind.
>
> ### Advantages
> (a) It, if successful, puts the A.F.V. in easy striking distance of the most appropriate objectives for their employment.
> (b) Surprise.
> (c) Would have a terrific moral effect on both German and French.
> (d) Could be most easily supported by infantry and R.E. (Royal Engineers).
> (e) Control and information will be from front to rear, and difficulties of co-ordination to surmount obstacles, and deal with resistance would be the more easily met.

It was further discussed that by landing on the main beach at Dieppe, the supply of ammunition for the tanks and stores for the engineers would be better co-ordinated, and that when it came to re-embarkation at the end of the raid, doing so at just one location would be the best choice as it would also help greatly with fighting a rear-guard action, which it was anticipated would be required.

It was also recognised that a head-on frontal attack on Dieppe harbour and its adjoining beaches had its 'disadvantages' because there were obstructions in the way which would require successful engineering work to displace them.

Lieutenant Colonel Mann also believed that such an attack had every prospect of success because the 'known' strength of the Dieppe garrison was 'only two companies of infantry not of the best quality, plus some divisional troops'.

It was clear that during the planning stages of the operation there were differing views as to whether a direct frontal assault on the centre of Dieppe was the right course of action to take. Despite this uncertainty, the plan approved by the Chiefs of Staff Committee on 13 May 1942 included the decision to carry out a frontal assault on the centre of the town.

The raid on Dieppe was significant, not just because it was the first time during the Second World War that such a large body of Canadian forces had seen action, but it was also the largest of the raids carried out by the Combined Operations section on occupied-Europe since the fall of France in 1940.

In the report's early paragraphs, Stacey speaks a great deal about the on-going struggle on the Eastern Front after Germany's invasion of Russia on 22 June 1941, at the beginning of what had been code-named Operation Barbarossa. To try to alleviate some of the devastation Russia had sustained following the German invasion, Stalin had been pushing his British and American allies to open up a Western Front.

On 8 September 1942, Churchill informed Parliament that the raid was a 'reconnaissance in force', with the object of getting 'all the information necessary before launching operations on a much larger scale.' It was, he said, 'an indispensable preliminary to full-scale operations'.

To this end, the report makes mention of a further speech made by Churchill in the House of Commons on 11 November 1942. Part of the speech included him reminding the House that in June 1942, the governments of the United Kingdom, the United States and Russia, had released a joint communique indicating that it was intended to open a second front in Western Europe some time in 1942, but that the main object of this announcement had been to deceive the Germans. Churchill added: 'In June I gave the Russian Government a written document, making it perfectly clear that while we were preparing to make a landing in 1942, we could not promise to do so.'

Point sixteen of the report provides some of the background for the raid on Dieppe, explaining how the idea for the raid was conceived as early as April 1942. This meant that the preparations and the planning for the operation, which at the time was still Rutter, were going ahead at a time when Prime Minister Churchill had stated that it was not absolutely certain an invasion of Western Europe, via a location somewhere along the French coast, would actually take place during the summer of 1942.

Point thirty-two of the report outlines the fact that, 'Intelligence reports indicate that Dieppe is not heavily defended', but there is no explanation as to how this information was obtained or what the referred to 'intelligence' actually was. Included in the same point are the raid's objectives, such as the destruction of German defences in the Dieppe area, along with similar installations at the airfield at Dieppe-St Aubin, located to the south of the town, as well as the radar station which was the specific target for Sergeant Jack Nissenthall. Other targets included power stations, dock and rail facilities, as well as petrol dumps. It was also proposed to remove German invasion barges believed to be in the town's harbour, and lastly to obtain secret documents from the German Divisional Headquarters, which was believed to be at Arques-la-Bataille, and to capture a number of German prisoners.

Point thirty-four of the report includes the fact that as well as the original intention for Rutter to use airborne troops to take out the coastal anti-aircraft batteries in the area, there had also been strong consideration for the use of glider-borne troops as well.

An important part of the original planning had included the use of a large number of aircraft from Bomber Command to carry out an aerial attack on the harbour during the earlier hours of the morning on the day of the attack, as well as the town's beach area, immediately before the amphibious landings. It was also planned that Allied aircraft would be present during the re-embarkation stage of the operation.

It certainly appears that the original planning for Operation Rutter was more professional and was better organised than what was eventually delivered under Operation Jubilee. If what had originally been ear marked for the raid on Dieppe had been provided, there is every chance that not only would the outcome have been completely different, but there would have also been far fewer casualties.

The bombing aspect of the operation was changed for Jubilee because of concern of over the potentially high number of French civilian casualties if targets on the ground could not be clearly identified by the bombers due to inclement weather. In conjunction with the proposed aerial bombing of Dieppe, there had also been a plan to carry out a diversionary night-time attack on Boulogne, but to prevent unnecessary civilian deaths this was changed to a day-time attack on the airfield at Abbeville.

The next part of the report covers the training aspect of the raid, and how the units allocated to take part began arriving at

Cowes on the Isle of Wight from 18 May onwards. These units began an intensive programme of physical training which was intended to toughen the men in readiness for the task ahead. The training for infantry soldiers included embarkation and beaching of landing craft, assault courses, unarmed combat, training in the use of Bangalore torpedoes, other weapons training, tactics, and speed marches. The engineers trained alongside the infantry units in assault work, while separate to this the tank battalion worked with the crews of the tank landing craft.

In relation to the physical condition of the Canadian soldiers, an interesting entry in the War Diary of the Headquarters, 2nd Canadian Division for the period ending 28 May 1942 reads as follows:

> Although the condition of the men is reasonably good, the assault courses and speed marches have shown that there is a great improvement to be made in this direction. In the speed marches, units are able to do five miles in 45 minutes but took between one and a half hours to two hours to do the remaining six miles. In the assault courses the men were able to complete the course but were, in many cases, unable to fight or fire effectively when finished.

After these failings had been pointed out to the separate units, and more gruelling and demanding training had been undertaken, fitness levels certainly saw an improvement, especially in such areas as the speed marches. But this aspect of the report concluded that although, 'the condition of the men has improved and better results have been secured from the speed marches, it has become evident that in the short time available, training to the standard required on a battalion basis is not possible without sacrificing valuable training.'

The report then moves on to a proposed exercise to put all the training carried out into practice. This exercise was known by the code name of 'Yukon', and was intended to begin on 10 June 1942. Troops from the Canadian 2nd Division acted as the assaulting force, with local troops acting as the German defenders. The plan was for the Canadian force to attack and destroy objectives at West Bay and Bridport on the Dorset coastline, which represented Dieppe, before re-embarking at West Bay and returning to Cowes on the Isle of Wight.

Exercise Yukon (see Chapter 2), took place over 11 and 12 June, but was far from satisfactory, let alone a success. The report explained how Lord Mountbatten, the man in charge of Combined Operations, had not seen the exercise as he had been away in America at the time and was therefore unable to properly or fairly assess who or what was ultimately responsible for the failings which had occurred. He therefore deemed that the best way forward was to postpone the live operation until a successful exercise had been completed. To this end, Yukon II took place between 22 and 24 June over the same terrain and at the same location as before. This time Mountbatten was present.

Even after Yukon II had taken place, there were still concerns about the lack of precision and time in bringing the landing craft to the particular beaches to which they had been allocated. There was also an issue with the smoke cover provided ahead of the landing craft arriving on the beaches. These matters were looked into in some detail by Lieutenant General Montgomery, and after they had been suitably addressed to his liking by 30 June, he announced he was happy for the operation to go ahead.

Operation Rutter was intended to commence on the night of 5 July, but this was put back because of the inclement weather due for that same evening. As it would remain unsettled for the following forty-eight hours, the next possible date the operation could commence was 8 July, but because of tidal issues this would mean troops would not be able withdraw from the beaches at Dieppe until 17.00 instead of the intended 11.00 as had originally been planned. If 8 July was not possible, 9 and 10 July were once again unsatisfactory because of tidal issues.

The realisation that there was no imminent chance of the operation going ahead saw its cancellation and the troops were disembarked and returned to their home stations.

On 14 July, surprising as it might seem, newspapers in Canada such as the *Globe* and *Mail* in Toronto, were allowed to publish reports about how Canadian forces had undergone intensive training as part of Combined Operations. Mr Ross Munro, a war correspondent from the Canadian Press, had been present throughout the men's training on the Isle of Wight and had written an accurate and detailed account of the training which had taken place. He did not mention any locations or the details of specific Canadian units.

What he had written had been scrutinised and passed by the British military censor.

The same news was reported in British newspapers on 16 July, with one of them, the *Daily Telegraph*, even naming some of the infantry units which had participated.

Stacey said in his report that the first reference he had found in relation to Operation Rutter being revived was on 14 July, in a note written by Lieutenant General McNaughton in his war diary about a discussion which had taken place about re-commencing the training which had previously taken place on the Isle of Wight.

On the afternoon of 16 July, discussions took place at a Force Commanders meeting which included the likes of General Roberts, Air Marshal Leigh Mallory and Captain Hughes-Hallett. Later the same day a separate meeting took place between General McNaughton, General Roberts and Vice Admiral Lord Louis Mountbatten. At both these meetings, the new operation, Jubilee, was discussed and agreed.

Stacey's report records that matters moved fairly quickly after this point, with a number of meetings taking place between concerned parties, and letters being sent between relevant individuals and separate branches of the military.

On 25 July, Mountbatten telephoned General McNaughton to inform him that, 'the Prime Minister and the War Committee of the Cabinet had approved Operation Jubilee in general principle: no date or place had been communicated to the Cabinet.'

Although attempts were made to keep details of the revival of the operation secret for as long as possible, an entry in the War Diary of the Royal Regiment of Canada dated 18 August 1942 shows that details of the raid were more widely known about than was possibly believed. The Commanding Officer of the regiment, the Adjutant, and the Company Commanders had known about the revival of the operation 'for the past ten days'. Major Law of the Camerons of Canada Regiment, and a similar group of his fellow officers, had known of the operation from 14 August.

To explain away the large movement of troops along the south coast of England, an order was issued from the Headquarters of the 2nd Canadian Division on 13 August 1942 detailing four military exercises known as Ford I, Ford II, Ford III, and Popsy, which were to last for a period of one month commencing on 15 August. The actual order to go ahead with the raid on Dieppe was only signed and issued on 17 August, the day before the operation began. It was only that same day that the decision not to carry out a preliminary aerial bombardment of German defences at Dieppe was made at a final meeting between Mountbatten and the three force commanders, which took place at RAF Tangmere.

Stacey's report concludes by listing the five different ports the regiments and vessels taking part in the raid left from, along with the names of both the regiments and the vessels concerned. It also records the fact that the number of officers and men who were allocated to take part in the raid totalled 6,106. This included eighteen members of No. 10 Commando (Inter-Allied) troops, although the Commando Veterans website records the number of men from this unit who took part in the raid as only being fifteen.

Once again, this in-depth report by Major Stacey pulls no punches and is as honest as he can possibly make it, despite some individuals potentially not being happy about him having done so. It is interesting to note that the British did not do anything of a similar nature, as the account of the raid they wished to promote was less to do with the truth and more about putting a positive spin on what, in essence, was a bad defeat, and the saving of certain military reputations.

CHAPTER SEVENTEEN

Canadian Military Report No. 142 – 18 July 1945

Report No. 142, dated 18 July 1945, is a 21-page report that was subsequently declassified on 9 September 1986. At that time, the following note was added to it: 'This is a preliminary narrative and should not be regarded as authoritative. It has not been checked for accuracy in all aspects, and its interpretations are not necessarily those of the Historical Section as a whole.'

The report is made up of some forty separate numbered paragraphs and also includes a number of appendices. Below are some of the more relevant entries. Some of the points are copied here verbatim, whilst others provide a flavour of their content.

Operation "Jubilee": The Raid on Dieppe, 19 Aug '42

Further New Information.

(1). A long series of reports has dealt with the Dieppe operation of 19 Aug '42. Those of most recent date

(Nos. 116, 128, 130) have recorded new information which has come to hand at various times from a number of sources, including repatriated prisoners of war. As a result of the victorious operations in North-West Europe in the spring of 1942, the remainder of the Canadian Dieppe prisoners have now been repatriated from Germany, and certain additional facts have thus become available.

It is clear that the compilation of this report could not have been completed effectively until all of those who had taken part in the raid, as well as those who had been captured, had returned to Canada and were able to provide their own personal perspective on the raid.

Paragraph three of the report makes reference to the meeting which had taken place between senior Canadian officers whilst held captive at Oflag VII-B prisoner of war camp on 13 September 1942, less than a month after they had been captured at Dieppe. The most senior of the officers present at that meeting was Brigadier William Wallace Southam, Commanding Officer, 6th Canadian Infantry Brigade.

The purpose of the meeting was to look at all aspects of the raid, good, bad or indifferent, whilst the events of 19 August 1942 were still fresh in the memory of those who had taken part. Out of this meeting came a report with observations about what had worked, what had gone wrong, and what could be improved upon in any future operations.

After his release at the end of the war, Brigadier Southam considered it important that attempts be made to locate the record of that meeting held on 13 September. He took it upon himself to contact the Canadian War Office in an effort to move this matter forward. One suggestion was to contact Lieutenant L.D. Lee of the Royal West Kent Regiment, who had not only been a prisoner at Oflag VII-B, but had been one of those who had attended the meeting in his capacity as camp secretary, and who had made a shorthand record of what had been said.

By chance, on his return to England, Lieutenant Lee had written to Brigadier Southam, and as a result of the brigadier's reply, Lieutenant Lee visited the Historical Section at Canadian Military Headquarters, where he was allowed to view his wartime notebook so that he could translate his own shorthand into a legible transcript, which was then included in the Appendix A.

Once Brigadier Southam had seen Lieutenant Lee's report and had viewed other accounts of the raid, he completed his own report, which focused on 'approach, landing, and subsequent events' (Appendix B).

Point six in Colonel Stacey's report is very succinct, and in an historical context, provides extremely sound advice.

> The documents attached hereto afford some interesting additions to our knowledge of the Dieppe operation. It is important to caution the Official Historian, however, against taking them in all respects precisely at their full-face value. It must be remembered that the officers who became prisoners of war were not in possession of the full facts concerning the results of the operation. (It may also be in order to record a remark made by Lieut. Lee: "Every P.W. is always extremely bitter.") Criticisms issuing from a prison camp are liable to be somewhat coloured by circumstances.

Lieutenant Lee is right, of course. Individuals rarely admit their failings or short comings in such a scenario, and sometimes, maybe even sub-consciously, slightly embellish the part they played and in some cases even recall events differently and incorrectly.

Colonel Stacey's next point in his report comments on Brigadier Southam's report on Dieppe.

> Brigadier Southam's own report does not greatly alter that account of the operation as it is already known. It throws additional light on the Brigadier's own activity, indicating in particular that the messages received from him to which references are made in report No.108 (paras 249 ff), were sent from "the remains of a scout car" of the 14th Canadian Army Tank Battalion.

To fully understand Colonel Stacey's report, the reader will need to know that the regiments which took part in the raid are referred to by him as a letter of the alphabet followed by the word "Battalion":

> "A" Battalion – South Saskatchewan Regiment
> "B" Battalion – Royal Regiment of Canada
> "C" Battalion – Royal Hamilton Light Infantry
> "D" Battalion – Essex Scottish Regiment
> "E" Battalion – Camerons of Canada
> "F" Battalion – Fusiliers of Mont-Royal

By way of showing some of the difficulties which can arise when compiling such a report, Colonel Stacey clarified certain events raised in some of the different reports compiled and submitted as being accurate accounts of the raid.

In the original report compiled from the recollections of the officers present at the meeting at Oflag VII-B on 13 September 1942, it was noted that Commandos on the left flank were attacked by German E-Boats 'as early as 02.00 hours'. Colonel Stacey points out that this claim is unsupported by any other evidence, and in paragraph twenty-four of Report No. 101, the Royal Navy reported the time of their first encounter with any German naval vessels as taking place at 03.47 hours.

Another ambiguity is the time at which the infantry support ships first came under enemy fire. The Oflag VII-B report puts the time as being 'by 03.40 hours'. This too is unsupported by any corroborating evidence other than that provided by Lieutenant Colonel R.R. Labatt in Report No. 128, who may well have contributed this information to the 'conference' at Oflag VII-B. In the absence of any other evidence, especially from naval sources, it is quite possible that Labatt was mistaken and that the suggested time of 03.40 is an error and did not take place.

Another bone of contention included in the initial report was whether or not the Germans were forewarned of the raid and had time to reinforce their defensive positions in and around Dieppe. This was certainly a widespread view shared amongst many returning POWs at the end of the war who had been captured at Dieppe, mention of which was recorded in Report No. 109. Despite these beliefs, that same report concluded the Germans did not have advanced information about the raid. Colonel Stacey posed the question that if the Germans had, in fact, been forewarned, why did it take them some five hours to get the bulk of their aircraft into the skies to assist their ground forces in defending Dieppe?

The closer Colonel Stacey examined the report that came out of the officer's conference at Oflag VII-B, the more inaccuracies he discovered. With respect to the number of British and Canadian troops who were successfully evacuated after the raid, the report stated that the belief was that 'only one platoon' of Camerons 'got away', but the actual numbers of Camerons who escaped and made it safely back to England were 265 officers and men. In the case of the Royal Hamilton Light Infantry, the Oflag VII-B report stated that, 'it is unlikely any of this battalion reached England'. In reality, however, 7 officers and 210 men returned.

Among the men who were captured at Dieppe, it was a commonly held belief that very few of the original attacking force returned to England. Brigadier Southam mentioned that, 'so much activity was seen offshore and so many landing craft were seen to have been hit or sunk that the men left behind felt that there could have been very few survivors'.

In relation to the Essex Scottish Regiment, the report stated that, 'No Naval craft came in to evacuate this battalion'. There is no known naval evidence which supports this narrative. The reality is that at least eight landing craft are known to have made it to Red Beach, where the men of the Essex Scottish were waiting to be evacuated, but six of these landing craft were subsequently destroyed.

With respect to the assault carried out by the men of the Royal Regiment of Canada on Blue Beach, the Oflag VII-B report strengthens the conclusion reached in Report No. 101, that 'the landing arrangements for this beach went badly awry'. It stated that the first wave of men of this regiment landed 35 minutes later than had been planned for, which differed from the naval report which stated that the first wave of men were just 17 minutes late in landing.

It is quite clear that if the Oflag VII-B report was used as a platform to provide a complete and accurate history of the raid on Dieppe, it would have completed an incorrect picture of what actually took place. Claims that 'tanks landed approximately on time' is not supported by any naval evidence. The claim that the Commanding Officer of the Fusiliers Marins Commando, Lieutenant Guy Vourch, was killed is also inaccurate.

Colonel Stacey's report also includes an account from Lieutenant J.E.R. Wood of the Royal Canadian Engineers, who was one of those captured at Dieppe. He was repatriated in spring 1945 from Oflag IV-C in Germany. Whilst held as a POW, Lieutenant Wood wrote an account of his part in the operation, a copy of which he made available to the History Section of the Canadian Military Headquarters.

On 19 August, Lieutenant Wood was on board Landing Craft LCT 3 when it landed on the beach at Dieppe: 'I crawled up for a look over the crest. Taking cover along the seawall in a shackling big anti-tank ditch about seven feet deep, were the infantry. The mechanical excavator was at one end. It must have been dug recently, concrete evidence of a break in security.'

It is interesting that Lieutenant Wood uses the presence of the ditch as 'evidence' that the Germans were forewarned of the Allied raid at Dieppe. Wood's evidence of the existence of a ditch across the beach is confirmed by other individuals. It has to be said that neither the presence of the ditch nor the digger is conclusive evidence that the Germans had prior knowledge of an imminent raid. Such an attack was possible anywhere along the entirety of the French coastline, the consequence of this was that the Germans were constantly improving and upgraded their defences because the disadvantage they had to deal with was not knowing when and where an eventual invasion would take place.

The following are additional notes made by Lieutenant Lee from the meeting at Oflag VII-B on 13 September 1942.

Dieppe

(1). The object of the Dieppe Operation was to carry out a large-scale raid; to capture and destroy beach and coastal defences, inland battery positions, aerodrome, harbour installations and to capture enemy invasion craft; the whole operation to be carried out in a space of time governed by the tides which was approximately eight hours. The days during which the operation could be carried out were from 18-23 August inclusive. The first five days would necessitate a two-tide operation, the last two a one-tide operation. An ancillary object was to draw out enemy naval and air force units.

Information

(2). Enemy. Information from air reconnaissance and ground sources indicated normal beach defences (wire at DIEPPE), no wire at PUITS, pillboxes, numerous anti-aircraft and field artillery positions and defended localities. 110 Division occupied the area. Reinforcements available. Armoured Division in vicinity of AMIENS. SS Hitler Division in vicinity of PARIS.

(3). Own troops taking part. Force Headquarters (2nd Canadian Division). Two infantry brigades (not war establishment – each battalion of 550 strength approximately due to physical limitation of naval craft). Tank battalion (Army), Royal Canadian Engineers detachment. Medical detachment. Provost detachment. Special Mortar and Medium Machine Gun detachments. Anti-Aircraft and Field Regiment detachments (to operate captured weapons). Military Commandos, Marine Commandos. Royal Navy and Military Beech Parties. Royal Air Force (Bomber, fighter). Royal Navy with personnel carrying and special craft.

Methods

(4). Landings were to take place on six beaches.

(a) at zero – Commandos to land on outer flanks under cover of darkness to destroy coast guns.

(b) at zero – Infantry battalions to land: "A" Battalion at POURVILLE, "B" Battalion at PUITS – surprise landing under cover of darkness. Task – "A" Battalion to secure POURVILLE and enable exploitation battalion to pass through, to secure radio direction-finding station and thereafter to hold north-west sector of DIEPPE beachhead being part of the outer perimeter to cover withdrawal. "B" Battalion to secure PUITS and the barracks there, high ground to east of PUITS and high ground to headland, east of DIEPPE which included heavy and light anti-aircraft positions, field battery positions and gas works, south of DIEPPE on river Argues, and then in to Brigade reserve in DIEPPE.

(c) at zero + 30 – two battalions to land on beach at DIEPPE each supported by one troop of tanks: Task – frontal attack on DIEPPE. Right battalion ("C" Battalion) to overcome beach defences, mop right half of DIEPPE, secure West Headland and BAMBETTA BARRACKS and establish perimeter defence on left of POURVILLE; left battalion ("D" Battalion) to overcome beach defences, mop left half of DIEPPE including any naval craft in harbour basin, secure military and naval headquarters in DIEPPE, then to secure race track south of DIEPPE and East Headland, establishing a perimeter defence from left of "C" Battalion to and including East Headland. With these battalions Royal Canadian Engineers personnel to land with demolition parties to blow sea wall and roadblocks, destroy enemy communications.

(d) at zero + 30 – "E" Battalion to land from "R" craft at POURVILLE and exploit through to destroy field battery, aerodrome and time permitting, enemy divisional headquarters at Arques-la-Bataille.

(e) at zero + 70 – Marine Commandos to enter harbour basin, secure area of harbour, take over naval headquarters and carry out certain demolitions in harbour area and secure enemy invasion craft for removal to England.

(f) at zero + 75 – Brigade Headquarters to land on DIEPPE beaches and establish themselves in DIEPPE. Additional troops to land, tanks and further detachments Royal Canadian Engineers to land at DIEPPE.

(g) remaining battalion ("F" Battalion) plus further tanks to stay afloat as reserve under force headquarters and subsequently for "F" Battalion to land and establish inner perimeter defence at DIEPPE.

(h) Royal Navy programme – to provide initial bombardment of DIEPPE front and West and East Headland followed by fire on request of Forward Observation Officer with each battalion, who had call on one destroyer.

(i) Royal Air Force programme – support of varying intensity throughout Operation commencing with bombing of defences (artillery positions) followed by smoking of East Headland and low flying attack of DIEPPE front, + 95 on request during Operation, close support and maintaining gradually receding bomb line around bridgehead on withdrawal.

(j) Royal Canadian Engineers – most comprehensive programme for destruction of dock installations, power house, rolling stock, communications, torpedo dump in caves East Headland, also to prepare demolition charges for each battalion to destroy enemy weapons.

(k) Administration and Quartermaster arrangements to include establishment of dumps in DIEPPE, medical evacuation scheme and provost control of beaches for withdrawal.

This was an extremely detailed operational plan, but the one thing it was clearly missing was a Plan B. There was absolutely no allowance for what to do if any of the eleven parts of the master plan did not work. As the old military saying goes, 'No plan survives first contact with the enemy'.

By way of example, there was clearly no understanding of whether the beach was made up of sand or pebbles, and if the latter, were they big or small? This had a major bearing on the entire raid, and undoubtedly led to large numbers of Allied deaths because the Churchill tanks that made it onto the beach could not get a grip with their tracks, and so could not support and protect the ground troops as was intended. The tanks literally became sitting ducks, with all their crews either being killed or captured.

The idea of carrying out a head-on frontal assault against a heavily defended harbour at Dieppe was almost suicidal. It is difficult to comprehend how anybody could have conceivably expected such a tactic to be successful, and even more surprising is that nobody involved in the planning of the operation challenged its competency.

It is apparent that the desire by senior Canadian military personnel to have their men "blooded" in action, and for the British authorities to acquiesce to their demands, was allowed to supersede basic common sense. To place such a large number of inexperienced and untested soldiers in a lead roll in such an operation was naïve to say the least.

The other oddity about this operation was that it did not serve any direct military purpose. With that in mind, it poses the question as to why there were so many elements included in the operational plan.

The rest of Lieutenant Lee's shorthand translated report covered what happened on the day. His was a more detailed and accurate account and was in no way an attempt at "sugar coating" or downplaying any aspect of it.

The Action Carried Out

As early as 02.00 hours, E-Boats attacked "R" craft (Commandos on left flank). Shortly after German Air Force dropped flares over infantry assault ships which came under fire by 03.40 hours from shore batteries. Exclusive right Commandos and "A" Battalion all units came under heavy fire while afloat and on the way in and suffered heavy casualties. Beach defences were greatly stronger than had been anticipated. There were further heavy casualties from intense enemy fire on landing due to additional medium machine guns [sic] (establish four companies). Elements of enemy reconnaissance battalion were observed well forward, and Germans state their defences were "Standing to" and had been for four days.

It is quite concerning to hear that the Germans had been anticipating a raid and had been in position to deal with such an eventuality for some four days. This may simply have been down to nothing more sinister than the fact that they, too, had heard the BBC broadcast which spoke of a forthcoming raid. Alternatively, did they have spies operating along the south coast of England who had noticed a build up of Allied shipping across the region's ports?

Commando on right secured surprise and carried out its task. "A" Battalion secured complete surprise on landing and on their right flank and gained all their objectives. On left flank were unable to capture the high cliff overlooking "A" Battalion beach. On being ordered to withdraw, succeeded in re-embarking seven L.C.A.s of troops. Time of re-embarking approximately 11.00 hours.

This confirms that Canadian forces were on French soil for at least nine hours. The reference to "A" Battalion was about the then acting Lieutenant Colonel Simon Fraser, more commonly referred to as Lord Lovat, who as the commanding officer of No. 4 Commando, led them during their successful campaign at Dieppe (See Chapter 10). Lord Lovat and the men of No. 4 Commando, who were the only Allied success of the Dieppe raid, had successfully knocked out the German gun battery they had been ordered to assault during the operation, and in doing so prevented the Germans from opening fire on other elements of the raiding party, as well as the Royal naval ships waiting out at sea.

The next section of the report makes for particularly painful reading, because putting aside the rights and wrongs of whether the raid should have ever taken place, it appears that C Battalion was, in essence, sent on a 'suicide mission'. Knowing the strength of the German defences they would have been faced with upon landing, it would not have been difficult to work out that potential casualties would be so high that there would be no point in landing where they did, especially in regards to what they had been tasked with doing once they were ashore. To add insult to injury, for those who made it off the beach, into the town and then back to the beach, they later perished having reached the comparative safety of their LCAs.

(7). Exploitation battalion encountered fire from cliff overlooking "A" Battalion beach on landing and suffered casualties, their Commanding Officer being killed. This Battalion made its way up west bank of river Scie to R.R. line, but was unable to cross to East and consequently withdrew, a number being re-embarked in L.C.A.s with "A" Battalion. Heavy casualties. It is believed only one platoon got away.

(8). "C" Battalion – sustained very heavy casualties from West Headland while afloat and on landing, came under fire at close range from eight pillboxes and two light artillery emplacements. The right company was practically wiped out after the capture of five pillboxes and the Casino. The battalion was too weak to attack the town although a small party entered the town remaining there for three and a half hours completely cut off. While in town this party mopped up streets in vicinity of Eglise St. Remy inflicting many casualties and destroying an enemy field gun. In all, some 45 enemy prisoners were taken and utilized as stretcher bearers in withdrawal. It is unlikely any of this battalion reached England as all L.C.A.s allotted to withdrawal, were destroyed by enemy fire.

(9). "D" Battalion – suffered first casualties on touchdown from intense medium machine gun fire on flanks followed by mortar fire. The Battalion landed considerably to right of its appointed place. Stretch of flat promenade about 200 yards in depth to buildings along front directly in front cover by medium machine gun and mortar fire. Companies could not get through wire on top of sea wall, heavy casualties following each attempt. One small party succeeded in entering town as far as harbour basin. Two lorries of enemy troops killed and numerous snipers in buildings. Companies finally too weak to attempt any further attack were ordered to hold beach until withdrawal. No naval craft came in to evacuate this battalion and it is believed none returned to England.

This reads worse than the previous section. There appears to have been absolutely no good reason for the men of D Battalion to have landed at all. This was borne out by the fact that not one of them made it back to England, having either been killed or captured.

(10). "B" Battalion – no surprise achieved – no preliminary bombardment or special fire laid on. Only part of three leading assault companies were landed in first wave and these were brought 35 minutes late by Navy. Remainder of companies finally reached beach nearly one hour late. Effect of darkness and smoke screen entirely lost. Contrary to "Intelligence" reports, wall covering beach heavily wired. Beach covered by medium machine gun fire from fortified house and pillboxes all along cliffs, also mortar and artillery. Succeeded in blowing gaps in wire but only twenty men and officers succeeded in reaching top of cliffs. Remainder were either killed or pinned on the beaches under the cliffs. Some wounded survivors may have reached England in a returning L.C.M. that had come into the beach late. Of 700 in battalion and attached troops, approximately 150 were taken prisoner.

The report also comments on the fact that Royal Marine Commandos had originally been tasked with entering the harbour at Dieppe, which in essence would have been a full frontal, suicidal attack. Common sense prevailed, however, and they were eventually landed on the same beach as F Battalion, where they were to assist moving all the battalions forward, off the beach, and into the town. However, like F Battalion, they suffered heavy casualties almost as soon as they disembarked from their landing craft. One of those killed was their Commanding Officer, Lieutenant Colonel Joseph Picton Phillips.

The final section of the report, item number sixteen, features the withdrawal plan:

Withdrawal Plan

The plan originally contemplated an outer and inner perimeter, the latter to be formed by "F" Battalion to enable the outer battalions to withdraw through a secure but limited beachhead, but this plan obviously did not come in to affect. The Force Commander appreciating withdrawal should be made at earliest possible moment, considering the tide, ordered withdrawal for 11.00 hours. No other orders came through as to withdrawal other than establishing zero. Apparently, the naval craft in the pool some several miles off shore waiting to take troops off were badly shot up because only a few L.C.A.s and L.C.T.s came in and these on the extreme right of DIEPPE beach with the exception of one L.C.T which came in on the left. Several were sunk before touching down, and L.C.A.s which did land to re-embark troops were so overcrowded that at least two sank on withdrawal. All the time they were machine gunned and under fire from heavy guns. Many were killed in the water. Smoke to be supplied by Air and Navy was inadequate and poorly timed to cover withdrawal, and no benefit was obtained from it.

It is interesting to note that each of the reports discussed in these chapters begins with what could be described as a "disclaimer":

> In the writing of this volume the author has been given full access to relevant official documents in possession of the Department of National Defence; but the inferences drawn and the opinions expressed are those of the author himself, and the Department is in no way responsible for his reading or presentation of the facts as stated.

The official documents referred to would have included thousands upon thousands of other documents, including war diaries, operational reports, regimental files, as well as miscellaneous papers covering numerous different related military subjects.

The main reason for the production of these reports was so that the Canadian public could have an authentic and comprehensive understanding of the part played by the Canadian military in the Second World War. Many of these reports were produced in the years immediately following the end of the war, some of which were available before the conclusion of events such as the Nuremberg Trials.

In essence, it could be argued that Canada's involvement in the Second World War, and the involvement of its forces in the Dieppe Raid, comes purely from the interpretation of just one man, but the source documents from which he has drawn his conclusions are publically available, so it is highly unlikely that Stacey would have been anything other than completely open and unbiased in his interpretation of the facts.

It could be argued that the Canadian reports were as accurate as they could have been at the time of writing, and were no doubt written as honestly as possible, but as more information came to light over time, however, it is harder to accept these original reports as definitive accounts of what happened at Dieppe.

CHAPTER EIGHTEEN

The Raid Seen Through 'Open Eyes'

In October 1996, Hugh G. Henry III, a student studying at St John's College, Cambridge, wrote a 383-page dissertation as part of his PhD. It was entitled, 'The Planning, Intelligence, Execution and Aftermath of the Raid on Dieppe, 19 August 1942.' The work contains some extremely interesting observations about the overall failings of the raid, along with whom it felt was responsible.

Before looking at the dissertation in more detail, it is useful to remind ourselves that the man in charge of Operation Rutter – the precursor to Operation Jubilee – was Lieutenant General Bernard Montgomery. He felt that when Rutter was postponed because of inclement weather, it should have been called off altogether because of the risk that the Germans had found out about it. The added dilemma as he saw it was that the thousands of men who were due to have taken part in it had already been briefed whilst on board their respective ships, and the chances of one of them not talking about it to a friend or relative before a revised version of it took place were slim.

It was Mountbatten who proposed that the operation should still go ahead, reasoning that even if the Germans had discovered there had been a plan to carry out an amphibious attack at Dieppe, the last thing they would expect would be for the same plan still to go ahead at a later date. There is a certain naivety attached to that way of thinking. Using a simple football comparison, it would be like saying because a player took a penalty and placed the ball high and to the right of the goalkeeper, there would be no expectation that he would do exactly the same thing the next time he took a penalty kick.

When the topic of the raid on Dieppe is discussed there is quite often a feeling of the "elephant in the room" scenario, especially when discussing Mountbatten's part in the organisation of the operation, and the fact that most historians, and other interested parties, see the raid as nothing other than a resounding defeat: an utter disaster that should never gone ahead. Despite this, there always appears to be a reluctance to mention Mountbatten in a negative manner, let alone proportion blame to him. In this dissertation, however, Henry goes beyond that and raises the issue of how Mountbatten went from being a captain in charge of a destroyer to being the man in charge of Combined Operations in just two years, something that had never previously been considered, certainly not for a man of ordinary standing on the ladder of social structure.

Henry's words, although written more than forty years after the event, and seventeen years after Mountbatten's murder by the IRA in 1979, are clear, precise and unambiguous. Even after his death Mountbatten was thought of fondly by the British public. Not only was he a relative of the British royal family, he was a favourite of Prince Charles, so to write about him in such terms could be described as a brave thing to do, even if the content of what was said was accurate.

Historically, the operation at Dieppe has always been seen as a disaster, especially from a Canadian perspective, and when such an event occurs there is a natural desire to proportion blame. In this case, the man who bore the brunt of it was Admiral Mountbatten. Henry clearly states in the first paragraph of his dissertation that Mountbatten had only been promoted to that rank because of his connections in high places, which by its very nature leads to the suggestion that his rank and military capabilities were not in line with each other, as maybe they should have been.

Here is what Henry had to say:

> In 1942 the newly formed Combined Operations Headquarters (COHQ) was responsible for mounting raiding operations and therefore directly responsible for the planning and execution of the Dieppe raid (code-named Operation *Jubilee*). The Chief of Combined Operations (CCO), Vice-Admiral Lord Louis Mountbatten, merely a captain of destroyers less than two years previously, owed his meteoric promotion to his ambition and connections in high places. Not only was he a close friend and like a son to Prime Minister Winston Churchill, but also cousin to King George V. Thus, on receiving the first reports of *Jubilee's* failure, Mountbatten was anxious to portray the operation in the best light possible. If the true extent of failure had become obvious at the time, his organisation and his position as CCO probably would have received so much criticism from the other three Services that COHQ and the position

of CCO would very likely have been abolished. Therefore, Mountbatten instigated immediate damage control in the form of propaganda to protect his organisation from criticism from the other Services and public opinion. The press and radio were inundated with headlines and stories claiming a great victory. These carried the themes of heroic deeds, success against overwhelming odds and, most important, that the huge casualties sustained were not in vain but justified by the 'lessons learned'. These 'lessons', the argument went, would be vitally important in planning future amphibious operations leading up to the eventual Allied invasion of Adolf Hitler's *Festung Europa*. The triumphant invasion of Normandy in 1944 reinforced what soon became regarded as fact, namely that valuable lessons learned on the Dieppe raid did not just contribute, but were indeed essential, to the success of D-Day. Mountbatten continued to consistently claim this long after the end of the war, to the point that many historians and veterans came to regard it as fact. This is reflected throughout the historiography. The official positive line was reinforced by politicians for their own reasons.

How interesting that the Canadian government, who as a result of the raid on Dieppe had seen their forces sustain the bulk of the casualties, were still prepared to support the official story that the raid had been nothing other than a success. Out of some 5,000 Canadian soldiers who had taken part in the raid, 3,367 of them had either been killed, wounded or captured. Put in another way, this was a casualty rate of 68 per cent, which by any standards was extremely high. Other than to protect public morale back home, it is hard to comprehend why the Canadian government took such a stance on the matter.

It is understandable that a man such as Mountbatten would wish to preserve his professional reputation in the aftermath of the raid, where the effectiveness of what he was ultimately responsible for was being questioned. What is unclear, however, is why so many others went along with the pretence that the raid had been nothing other than a success.

Hugh Henry's dissertation continues as follows:

> The Canadian government was quick to realise the need for some kind of public explanation of the operation, particularly in relation to the high casualty figures. Therefore, on 27 August 1942, the Commander-in-Chief, First Canadian Army Overseas, Lieutenant-General Andrew G.L. McNaughton, received the following cable.
>
> *There is a feeling that the public ought to have some sort of authoritative statement in the form of a white paper or similar document prepared by Canadian Army or CMHQ* [Canadian Military Headquarters, London] *in which the participation of the Canadians at Dieppe is dealt with in a factual way as a military operation from the time they left England, until they returned with some indication of the preparation necessary.*

As discussed in previous chapters, the Historical Officer at Canadian Military Headquarters (CMHQ) was Major Charles P. Stacey. After approval of the initial report by the relevant

Canadian authorities, it was passed on to COHQ, which requested certain sections be cut.

Mountbatten's insistence on the revision of this white paper is a prime example of the effect and influence he had, both during the war and after, on the recording of events and later historical writing. Therefore, it is instructive to recount this case in detail.

The content of the following paragraph of Hugh Henry's dissertation is truly remarkable:

> During the operation the Germans had captured the military operational order, over which, in Stacey's words, Mountbatten had shown some disgust ... and had ruled that nothing was to be published that would in any way tend to admit the loss. At the same time, Mountbatten reportedly remarked something to the effect, 'even Boy Scouts knew better than that'. (This ignores the fact that the order itself, approved by CCO, authorized each brigade headquarters to carry two copies ashore.)

The fact that such an action took place is simply incredible. The only point that is not covered was when the copy of the operational order was recovered by the Germans. If it was found after the battle was over, it could be argued that this would not really make that much difference. However, if it had been discovered whilst the fighting was going on, it could have not only determined the outcome of the raid, but also led to more Allied soldiers dying than otherwise might have done so.

Hugh Henry's dissertation continues to say:

The task of revising the draft at COHQ was given to an American, Major Jock Lawrence, who a few months earlier had worked for Metro-Goldwyn-Mayer in Hollywood, California. His draft was unacceptable for issuance by the Canadian Government and Stacey was again ordered to redraft it, to which Mountbatten, Stacey says, 'To end a long story briefly ... finally gave his blessing'.

The cuts insisted by Mountbatten resulted in an extremely watered-down version of events and it is worth noting that the following information was excised: the operation's local objectives; details about the decision to withdraw; a reference that many of the planned objectives were not attained; comments on pre-raid training; and the names of all British commanders (although the Canadian unit commanders were permitted to remain).

Stacey concludes this section with comments on the command arrangement, which deserve quoting in full, as it later became a point of historical controversy:

> I had written, 'The whole operation was under the general supervision, and the plans were subject to the approval, of Vice-Admiral Lord Louis Mountbatten GCVO, DSO, Chief of Combined Operations. Canadian plans were concerted with the latter by Lieutenant-Colonel H.D.G. Crerar, DSO, General Officer Commanding a Canadian Corps'. As published,

this meant Canadian plans were concerned with the Chief of Combined Operations (Vice-Admiral Lord Louis Mountbatten, GCVO, DSO), by Lieutenant-General H.D.G. Crerar, DSO, General Officer Commanding a Canadian Corps'. The Canadian reader was thus denied any real understanding of the important part played by Lord Louis and his headquarters in the affair.'

Commenting on Major Lawrence, Stacey writes: 'In retrospect, it seems perhaps not altogether unsuitable that a man who had done publicly for Sam Goldwyn should now be doing publicity for Dickie Mountbatten'. Stacey continued that, 'Putting an American on the job was, to say the least, extraordinarily tactless. At the time I suspected it of being a calculated insult. Now, I am inclined to think it was just an exceptional piece of stupidity.' Stacey's notes at the time state that, 'He had cut out many facts and substituted adjectives; his draft was in terms which could not be issued by the Canadian Government.'

The obvious question which has to be asked of Hugh Henry's dissertation is, does it suggest a cover up took place to try to hide the complete facts about the raid on Dieppe from the British and Canadian public, whether for sound military and/or political reasons, which would be in keeping with, and expected, during a time of war? Or, was it more about simply saving an individual's military reputation and career?

The British public had already seen negative outcomes throughout those early years of the war which could not have helped but negatively effect morale amongst the civilian population. During April and May 1940, British forces had been defeated at Namsos in Norway, as Germany fought to secure the flow of much needed iron ore deposits from mines at Kiruna in the north of Sweden to Germany's war industries.

The British Expeditionary Force had been soundly defeated in Europe and forced back to the French coast at Dunkirk in May 1940, where they had only escaped by the skin of their teeth due in the main to Churchill's positivity and the professionalism of the British Royal Navy.

The raid on Dieppe had clearly been a defeat for the British and Canadians, of that there is no question. From a political sense, it certainly did not suit the British government to have to present yet another negative outcome to the British public, so putting a positive spin on the events, and losses, at Dieppe, would have undoubtedly been an attractive proposition for them. When such losses occur it is not uncommon for individuals to be held responsible: Dieppe was no different. People wanted answers, especially as there was a question mark over the reasons for why the raid took place. On this occasion, the man in the firing line was Louis Mountbatten. His reputation was quite clearly at stake, and the part he played in the planning of the raid still remains a bone of contention, especially in the eyes of the families of the Canadians who took part in it.

Hugh Henry's complete dissertation can be read in full at www.repository.cam.ac.uk.

CHAPTER NINETEEN

Beach Comber the Homing Pigeon

Animals of all descriptions have been used in war for hundreds of years. The First World War, for example had relied heavily on horses, not just for transport purposes, but because cavalry units were initially still considered to be the mainstay of British offensive military tactics.

Although pigeons had been used during the First World War, by the time of the Second World War it was these birds, specifically the homing variety, who had a vital role to play. Indeed, such was their importance that Britain formed its own Air Ministry Pigeon Section, part of which was the Pigeon Policy Committee, who made decisions over pigeon use and deployment.

Besides their ability to fly at speed, pigeons have an innate homing ability which made them the obvious choice to use when the need arose for the delivery of urgent messages.

Throughout the 1930s, pigeon racing was a popular pastime amongst the British public, with thousands of pigeon fanciers belonging to numerous clubs and organisations across the country. With the outbreak of war, and with concerns growing over the ability to be able to feed them, thousands of owners donated their birds to the newly formed National Pigeon Service, which was a civilian volunteer organisation.

The Army, Royal Air Force, Home Guard, the police, and even Bletchley Park used pigeons as part of their means of communication. Such was their importance to the Allied war effort, that the killing, wounding, or 'molesting' of homing pigeons was designated an offence under Regulation 21A of the Defence of the Realm Act. Anyone found doing so faced a six-month prison sentence or a £100 fine.

On the morning of 19 August 1942, Senior Canadian Army officers waiting anxiously at their headquarters in London for news of the raid, were notified that their troops had landed at Dieppe not by a phone call, radio message, or dispatch rider, but by a note attached to a pigeon's leg.

The pigeon in question was called Beach Comber, or to give it its official service number, NPS.41.NS.4320. The pigeon had been bred by Mr W. Lane, from Ipswich, Suffolk, and at the outbreak of the war had become part of the National Pigeon Service. Prior to Dieppe, Beach Comber had completed a number of training flights from such places as Berwick, Belfast and Penzance.

The journey from Dieppe to London is a distance of approximately 150 miles 'as the crow flies', and with pigeons having the ability to travel at an average speed of at least 50 miles per hour, it is a journey that would have taken Beach Comber a minimum of around 3 hours to complete. It would not have been an easy journey: having initially made his way through the mist and smoke covering the beaches at Dieppe, Beach Comber would have made his way across the English Channel, avoiding aircraft, bullets, and explosions as he went.

Beach Comber was actually one of two pigeons who were released by Allied forces at Dieppe, the other bird, whose name is unfortunately lost to history, did not make it back home.

The Dickin Medal, often referred to as the animal equivalent of the Victoria Cross, was first introduced in 1943 by Maria Dickin, a social reformer and a pioneer of animal welfare, who in 1917 founded the People's Dispensary for Sick Animals (PDSA). The medal was intended to commemorate the work of animals during the Second World War. It was, and still is, awarded to animals who have displayed 'conspicuous gallantry or devotion to duty whilst serving with, or were associated with, any branch of the Armed Forces or Civil Defence Units'. The award comes in the form of a bronze medal and bears the words, 'For Gallantry' and 'We Also Serve' surrounded by a laurel wreath. It hangs on a striped ribbon of green, dark brown, and pale blue.

It was first awarded in December 1943 to three pigeons allocated to the RAF, who had saved the lives of airmen whose aircraft had ditched in the sea. Without the birds flying back to their station, the location of the downed airmen might never have been known in time for them to be rescued. Between 1943 and 1949, the medal was awarded a total of fifty-four times and commemorated thirty-two pigeons, eighteen dogs, three horses, and even a ship's cat.

On 6 March 1944, the PDSA awarded Beach Comber the Dickin Medal for his historic flight from Dieppe to London on 19 August 1942. The citation read as follows: 'For bringing the first news to this country of the landings at Dieppe, under hazardous conditions in August 1942, while serving with the Canadian Army.'

Beach Comber remains the only 'Canadian' war pigeon to have ever been awarded a Dickin Medal, and is one of only three animals ever to receive this prestigious award whilst serving with Canadian forces. (The other two are Sam, a German Shepherd, and a Newfoundland called Gander.)

Conclusion

The events at Dieppe on 19 August 1942 still cause discussion and disagreement about its purpose and planning. It is always easy to debate such matters many years after they have actually taken place, and to make comments about who won, or whether things could have turned out differently if things had been done another way.

War, by its very nature, is a murky business where things very rarely go completely as planned. The fact that people, both military and civilian, are killed is part of any conflict. But if human life is to have any value, which it must, then there must be a correlation between the operational requirement to attack a designated military target and the anticipated losses required to achieve it. For some reason, this did not take place at Dieppe.

The planning for the Dieppe Raid was poor. Was this because it was rushed for political reasons, or was it because of the ineptness of certain individuals who were involved in putting the operation together? One argument put forward for the raid going ahead was for the Allied need to appease Stalin, who wanted an invasion of Nazi-occupied Western Europe in the hope that it would help relieve the pressure on Soviet forces trying to prevent their country being overrun by Germany. With both British and American forces heavily committed in the Far East and North Africa, any kind of invasion of occupied Europe was never realistically going to take place in the timeframe that Stalin wanted it to. The real worry for the Allies was that if they did nothing, then Stalin may have decided his best option was to seek some kind of agreement with Germany to end the fighting, which would have then released hundreds of thousands of Nazi troops to switch their attention to Western Europe, potentially making any subsequent Allied invasion nigh on impossible.

With a full-scale invasion of Europe a definite future proposition, consideration had to be given as to how such an event would materialise. One answer was a raid such as the one that took place at Dieppe.

The very nature of such a raid meant it was going to be extremely difficult and dangerous, so utilising battle-hardened, experienced troops should have played a pivotal role in the planning, especially if it was to have any realistic chance of being successful. The fact that out of the raiding force of 6,000 Allied soldiers, some 5,000 were inexperienced and untested Canadian soldiers, not to mention that there was little in the way of artillery support from the Royal Navy, and that the Allies did not have control of the skies above Dieppe, begs the question: what did the planners of the operation think was going to happen? Add to this that out of the twenty-seven Churchill tanks which made it onto the beach, only fifteen of them made it into the town. This was largely due to bad intelligence about the make up of the beach, which was composed of pebbles rather than sand. All of the tank crews were subsequently either captured or killed in the raid.

In essence, it could be said that the Dieppe Raid went ahead to appease both Stalin and the Canadian government and their military authorities. Knowing there would be little in the way of artillery or air support, the decision was taken to place large numbers of inexperienced Canadian soldiers front and centre so that if casualties were high, the risk of upsetting the British public would be greatly reduced. As for the Canadians, 900 of their men were killed, hundreds more were wounded, and 1,946 were captured and became POWs. The Canadian people would never forget the disaster of Dieppe, and they would certainly never forgive the incompetence of those involved in planning the ill-fated raid.

On Tuesday, 8 September 1942, just three weeks after the raid on Dieppe, a debate in the Houses of Parliament took place entitled 'The War Situation'. It was opened by a rather lengthy address by Prime Minister Winston Churchill, and included the following comments:

> The second important operation was the attack upon Dieppe. It is a mistake to write of this as "a Commando raid," although some Commando troops distinguished themselves remarkably in it. The military credit for this most gallant affair goes to the Canadian troops, who formed five-sixths of the assaulting force, and to the Royal Navy, which carried them all there and which carried most of them back. The raid must be considered as a reconnaissance in force. It was a hard savage clash such as are likely to become increasingly numerous as the War deepens.

> We had to get all the information necessary before launching operations on a much lager scale. This raid, apart from its reconnaissance value, brought about an extremely satisfactory air battle in the

West which Fighter Command wish they could repeat every week. It inflicted perhaps as much loss upon the enemy killed and wounded as we suffered ourselves. I, personally, regarded the Dieppe assault, to which I gave my sanction, as an indispensable preliminary to full-scale operations.

I do not intend to give any information about these operations, and I have only said as much as I have because the enemy can see by his daily reconnaissances [sic] of our ports many signs of movements that we are unable to conceal from his photography. He is also aware of the steady and rapid influx into this island of United States' divisions and other troops, but what he does not know is how, when, where and with what forces and in what fashion he will be smitten. And on this point, it is desirable that he should be left to his own ruminations, unassisted by British or American advice or comment.

It is quite clear that Churchill was being rather cagey with his choice of words, possibly so as not to provide the German High Command with anything that might be of strategic value or to provide them with any information which could be used for propaganda purposes.

When Churchill said, 'I, personally, regarded the Dieppe assault, to which I gave my sanction, as an indispensable preliminary to full-scale operations', was this an effort to publicly support and help protect the reputation of Louis Mountbatten, the person who would have otherwise been blamed for the Allied losses at Dieppe?

I feel compelled to mention again the story surrounding Jack Nissenthall. Putting emotion to one side, what he did at Dieppe undoubtedly saved the lives of many people throughout the remaining years of the war, and the fact that he received no official recognition for what he did is scandalous. This is a man who, despite being an extremely important asset to the Allies in the field of radar technology, volunteered and was allowed to undertake a mission that would result in him taking a cyanide capsule in the event of his capture.

It is completely understandable that whilst the war was still going on, his actions were kept secret, but once the war was over, why he was not officially recognised for what he did is almost criminal.

While the Dieppe Raid is, understandably, considered a failure, some positives could be taken from it, and some lessons were most definitely learned.

Communications during the raid between the different units from the Army, Navy and RAF were far from acceptable and highlighted their importance in such a fast-moving theatre.

A good example of this failure was a decision taken by Canadian Major General John Hamilton Roberts, Officer Commanding 2nd Canadian Infantry Division, who during the raid was on board his command vessel, HMS *Calpe*. Unable to make radio contact with his troops who had already made it ashore, and unable to see them physically because of heavy Allied smoke deployed across the beach, he took the decision to commit his reserve troops, Les Fusiliers Mont-Royal and elements of the Royal Marines, into the affray. By doing so, he inadvertently increased the number of Canadian casualties.

At 07.00, the Fusiliers began making their way towards their allocated beach. No sooner had they begun their journey than they were engaged by the Germans. Most of the landing craft were destroyed or put out of action before they reached the beach, and from those that did, only a few men then managed to reach the town. To make matters even worse, Roberts then ordered his other reserve unit, the Royal Marines to land on the same beach in order to support the Fusiliers. There was an unfortunate delay in this order being carried out because the Royal Marines were not ready to disembark into the waiting landing craft. It was a disaster. On their way into their designated beach, they also came under heavy German fire, with many of the landing craft destroyed or disabled before they even made it to the shore. Those who did were either killed or captured.

On recognising the dire situation he and his men were in, Lieutenant Colonel 'Tigger' Phillipps, the Marines' commanding officer, stood upon the stern of his landing craft and signalled for the rest of his men to turn back. He was killed a few moments later.

The Mulberry harbours, which would prove to be an integral part of the D-Day landings at Normandy two years after Dieppe, came about as it was realised that attempting to capture a well-defended seaport with the intention to use it as a bridgehead, as happened at Dieppe, simply left too much to chance. If landing forces failed to capture the harbour, then any invasion could flounder and fail at that point.

The raid on Dieppe showed just how important aerial and naval bombardments of enemy defensive positions were prior to amphibious landings taking place. This was despite the fact that the very act of bombarding enemy positions would likely indicate to the enemy that an amphibious assault was imminent.

Whenever a historian carries out an analysis of the raid on Dieppe, training is rarely mentioned, but its importance cannot be emphasised enough. Every possible scenario of such events had to be taken seriously. They had to be as realistic as possible and practised methodically so that it almost became second nature. The tougher the training was, the more chance there was that the operation would achieve a successful conclusion. The fact that Dieppe was far from being a success speaks volumes about the quality of the training the men were put through in preparation for the raid.

It would be true to say that lessons were learned from the raid on Dieppe, but this can also be said of any such operation. Lessons can always be learned because no two operations are ever the same. Different elements will always come in to play depending on different factors, such as weather conditions, location, size of raiding party, training and planning for the operation, the time of the year it takes place, experience, and size of enemy forces, to name but a few.

One result of the Dieppe raid was the understanding for much greater initial air and naval bombardments to support the troops tasked with landing on the beach. Having said that, it surely did not need the raid on Dieppe to take place for this to be discovered.

Another less than ideal aspect of the raid was the decision to conduct a full-on frontal assault on certain beaches. Once again, there was surely no need to carry out the raid just to discover a large number of casualties would be sustained as the result of such an action. Trench warfare in the First World War had shown that brave young men running across no-man's-land towards heavy machine guns would result in extremely high casualty numbers. Indeed, such a tactic had been deployed on the first day of the Battle of the Somme and resulted in a staggering 57,470 British casualties, including 19,240 fatalities.

With the benefit of hindsight, why the Queen's Own Cameron Highlanders of Canada had been tasked with making their way some 5 miles inland to reach their objective, which was to meet up with the tanks of The King's Own Calgary Regiment and capture the airfield at Saint-Aubin-sur-Scie, is a mystery. Even in ideal conditions, with no obstacles or enemy trying to block their way, it is a journey that would have taken them at least 1 hour and 15 minutes each way to complete. But making that journey whilst having to fight against a well-established enemy was a totally different scenario.

Of the 503 Cameron Highlanders who took part in the raid, 346 became casualties: 60 were killed in action; 8 died of their wounds after they had been evacuated; 167 were captured and became prisoners of war, 8 of whom died of their wounds. Of the 268 who returned to England, 103 were wounded. A total of 25 Cameron Highlanders were decorated for their actions at Dieppe. The regiment received two Distinguished Service Orders (the second highest award for bravery for officers after the Victoria Cross), two Military Crosses, three Distinguished Conduct Medals (the second highest award for bravery for non-commissioned members after the Victoria Cross), four Military Medals, thirteen Mentions in Dispatches and a Croix de Guerre with bronze palms. One of the Distinguished Service Order recipients was the acting commanding officer, Major Law.

Raids such as the one at Dieppe are dependant to a large extent on the element of surprise, especially if they are to have any chance of succeeding. The landings at Dieppe were anything but a surprise, with many of those who died or were wounded never actually making it ashore, while for those who did, many never made it off the beach. With the element of surprise having been lost even before the landings took place, there is a solid argument to be had that the raid should have been called off at that time.

What is hard to fathom is how an operation planned by experienced military men, who by the very nature of their senior ranks were far from being stupid or inept individuals, contained so many obvious flaws, which surely must have been obvious to these men at the time. Did basic common sense simply get lost amongst the various political and military demands of war, which sometimes does not place the premium price on life that it should have?

By the time the last troops were withdrawn at 14.00, Allied losses in men and equipment were 907 Canadians killed, 586 wounded and 1,946 taken prisoner. A total of 45 British Commandos and Royal Marines were killed, with a further 197 either wounded or captured. The Royal Navy lost 1 destroyer along with 33 landing craft, whilst suffering 550 dead and wounded. The RAF, meanwhile, lost 106 aircraft.

In summary, the only real lessons to have come out of the failings of Dieppe were the need for much better planning and better communications. Everything else, such as training, better air and naval gun support, specialised landing craft, and a thorough reconnaissance of the proposed landing sites, should have been expected.

The Allied defeat at Dieppe became a textbook example of how not to undertake an amphibious landing, and helped lay the framework for the Normandy landings in June 1944. Dieppe also showed the importance and necessity of keeping the element of surprise for as long as possible. Not only did this allow as many men of the attacking force to get ashore as possible, but it also delayed the German defenders from opening fire. There was clearly a need for an aerial bombardment of the German defensive batteries prior to the raiding parties coming ashore. However, concerns over civilian casualties were allowed to outweigh the safety of the thousands of men who took part in the raid, and with that the overall effectiveness of the raid was potentially compromised.

An ineffective tactic from the First World War that resulted in enormous numbers of Allied casualties was the one that saw brave young men charging blindly across no-man's-land head first towards the enemy trenches. The results were catastrophic. Despite this, one of the tactics deemed suitable to deploy at Dieppe by the planners of the operation was a full-frontal assault against the town's heavily defended port area. Sadly, it took the heavy losses which came about at Dieppe to ensure that such a tactic was not used again.

Whilst it is accepted that Canadian forces fought bravely in the face of a determined and heavily armed enemy, it would be fair to say that even battle-hardened and experienced soldiers would have faired no better at Dieppe, which to a large degree was brought about by the ineptitude of the senior officers who were involved in the planning of the operation. For some inexplicable reason, they were of the belief that despite the tactics they had decided to deploy, casualties would be relatively low. However, as the facts of the raid unfortunately show, they were wrong.

The failings at Dieppe directly led to the design and construction of Mulberry harbours that were used to great effect during the D-Day landings, after planners realised that their previous belief of the need to capture a major port to be able to establish a second front was wrong. More research was also carried out into beaches and their structure so that vehicles subsequently brought ashore were, when required, adapted accordingly and could be an effective part of the raid.

It would be fair to say that despite the failings at Dieppe, of which there were many, lessons were quickly learned and future wartime amphibious landings consequently had every chance of succeeding.

APPENDIX A

Forces Deployed at Dieppe

Ground Forces

Commander – Major General John Roberts, 2nd Canadian Infantry Division

2nd Canadian Infantry Division

4th Canadian Infantry Brigade – Brigadier Sherwood Lett

- The Essex Scottish Regiment
- The Royal Hamilton Light Infantry
- The Royal Regiment of Canada

5th Canadian Infantry Brigade

- Three platoons of The Black Watch (Royal Highland Regiment) of Canada
- Mortar Platoon of The Calgary Highlanders

6th Canadian Infantry Brigade – Brigadier William Southam

- Les Fusiliers Mont-Royal (Floating Reserve)
- The Queen's Own Cameron Highlanders of Canada
- The South Saskatchewan Regiment
- No. 6 Defence Platoon (Lorne Scots)

14th Army Tank Regiment (The Calgary Regiment [Tank])

Detachment of 3rd Light Anti-Aircraft Regiment, Royal Canadian Artillery (RCA)

Detachment of 4th Field Regiment, RCA

The Toronto Scottish Regiment (Machine Gun)

- No. 3 Commando (British Army), Lt-Col John Durnford-Slater
- No. 4 Commando (British Army), Lt-Col Simon Fraser, 15th Lord Lovat
- No. 10 Inter-Allied Commando (French speakers attached to other units as interpreters), Lt Col Dudley Lister
- A Company, No. 40 Commando Royal Marines, Lt Col Joseph Picton 'Tigger' Phillipps
- No. 30 Commando (intelligence gathering)

In addition, a detachment of the 1st US Ranger Battalion was assigned as observers to various units.

Naval Forces

Commander – Captain John Hughes-Hallett, RN

Eight Hunt-class destroyers

- *Albrighton* – Lt Ronald John Hanson, RN
- *Berkeley* – support to *Calpe*, controlled low fighter cover squadrons under Act Sqd Ldr J.H. Scott, also "First Rescue Ship"
- *Bleasdale* – Lt Peter Barthrop North Lewis, RN
- *Brocklesby* – Lt Cdr Edward Nigel Pumphrey, DSO, DSC, RN

- *Calpe* – Headquarters ship – Lt Cdr John Henry Wallace, RN
- *Fernie* – reserve Headquarters ship – Lt Herbert Bernard Acworth, RN
- *Garth* – Lt Cdr John Percival Scatchard, RN
- ORP *Slazak* (Polish Navy) Lt Cdr Romuald Nalecz-Tyminski, ORP
- HMS *Locust* – gun boat, "Cutting Out Force" carrying RM Commandos – Cdr Robert Edward Dudley Ryder, VC, RN
- 9th Minesweeper Flotilla
- 13th Minesweeper Flotilla

Nine landing ships, infantry each with a number of landing craft

- HMS *Duke of Wellington* - Landing Ship, Infantry (Hand-Hoisting)
- HMS *Glengyle* - Landing Ship, Infantry (Large)
- HMS *Invicta* - Landing Ship, Infantry (Small)
- HMS *Prince Charles*
- HMS *Prince Leopold*
- HMS *Princess Beatrix* - Landing Ship, Infantry (Medium)
- HMS *Princess Astrid*
- HMS *Prins Albert*
- HMS *Queen Emma*

Supporting elements from Royal Navy Coastal Forces

- 12 Motor Gun Boats
- 4 Steam Gun Boats of the 1st SGB Flotilla
- 20 Motor Launches

Air Forces

Commander – Air Vice Marshal Trafford Leigh-Mallory
  Deputy Senior Air Staff Officer Group Captain Harry Broadhurst flew "air observation" at Dieppe.

- 11 Group RAF Fighter Command
  - 48 Spitfire Squadrons
    - No. 19 Squadron, RAF Fowlmere
    - No. 41 Squadron, RAF Merston
    - No. 43 Squadron, RAF Acklington
    - No. 64 Squadron RAF, Spitfire IX, RAF Hornchurch
    - No. 66 Squadron, RAF Ibsley
    - No. 71 Squadron RAF (one of the three "Eagle Squadrons" flown by Americans in the RAF), RAF Gravesend
    - No. 81 Squadron, RAF Hornchurch
    - No. 87 Squadron, RAF Charmy Down
    - No. 91 Squadron, RAF Hawkinge
    - No. 111 Squadron, RAF Kenley
    - No. 121 (Eagle) Squadron, RAF Southend
    - No. 122 Squadron, RAF Hornchurch
    - No. 124 Squadron, RAF Spitfire HF VI RAF Biggin Hill
    - No. 129 Squadron, RAF Leconfield
    - No. 130 Squadron, RAF Portreath
    - No. 131 Squadron, RAF Atcham
    - No. 133 (Eagle) Squadron, RAF Lympne
    - No. 134 Squadron, RAF Baginton
    - No. 154 Squadron, RAF Hornchurch
    - No. 165 Squadron, RAF Eastchurch
    - No. 222 Squadron, RAF Hornchurch

- No. 232 Squadron, RAF Debden
- No. 242 Squadron, RAF Turnhouse
- 302 "City of Poznan" Polish Fighter Squadron, RAF Jurby
- 303 "Kosciuszko" Polish Fighter Squadron, RAF Northolt
- 306 "City of Torun Polish Fighter Squadron, RAF Church Fenton
- 308 "City of Krakow Polish Fighter Squadron, RAF Northolt
- No. 310 (Czechoslovak) Squadron, Spitfire Vb, RAF Perranporth
- No. 312 (Czechoslovak) Squadron, Spitfire, Vb, RAF Harrowbeer
- No. 317 "City of Wilno" Polish Fighter Squadron, Spitfire Vb, RAF Acklington
- No. 331 (Norwegian) Squadron, Spitfire Vb, RAF North Weald
- No. 332 (Norwegian) Squadron, Spitfire Vb, RAF North Weald
- No. 340 (GC/IV/2 *Ile de France*) (French), Spitfire Vb, Hornchurch, RAF Biggin Hill
- No. 350 (Belgian), Squadron, Spitfire Vb, RAF Debden
- No. 401 Squadron RCAF, RAF Biggin Hill
- No. 403 Squadron RCAF, RAF Baginton
- No. 411 Squadron RCAF, RAF Hornchurch
- No. 412 Squadron RCAF, RAF Digby
- No. 416 Squadron RCAF, RAF Peterhead
- No. 501 Squadron RAF, RAF Kenley
- No. 602 Squadron RAF, RAF Renfrew
- No. 610 Squadron RAF, RAF Westhampnett

- No. 611 Squadron RAF, RAF Kenley
- No. 616 Squadron RAF, RAF Kirton-in-Lyndsey
  - Eight squadrons for ground attack
    - No. 3 Squadron RAF Hurricane IIC, RAF Stapleford Tawney
    - No. 32 Squadron RAF Hurricane IIB, IIC, RAF Acklington
    - No. 43 Squadron RAF Hurricane, RAF Tangmere, Danny Le Roy du Vivier (Belgian)
    - No. 87 Squadron RAF Hurricane, RAF Charmy Down
    - No. 174 Squadron RAF Hurricane, RAF Manston
    - No. 175 Squadron RAF Hurricane, RAF Dunsfold
    - No. 245 Squadron RAF Hurricane, RAF Hawkinge
    - No. 253 Squadron RAF Hurricane, RAF Kirton-in-Lindsey
  - Three Typhoon Hawker squadrons
    - No. 56 Squadron RAF, RAF Snailwell
    - No. 266 Squadron RAF Typhoon IB, RAF West Malling
    - No. 609 Squadron Typhoon IB, RAF West Malling
- RAF Army Cooperation Command, No. 35 Wing
  - No. 26 Squadron RAF – Mustang I, RAF Gatwick
  - No. 239 Squadron RAF - Mustang I, RAF Lindholme
  - No. 400 Squadron RCAF - Mustang I, W/Cdr Waddell, RAF Odiham

- No. 414 Squadron RCAF - Mustang I, W/Cdr Begg
- RAF Army Cooperation Command, No. 36 Wing, RAF Croydon
  - No. 13 Squadron RAF Bristol Blenheim light bomber (laying smoke), RAF Odiham
- RAF Army Cooperation Command, No. 32 Wing
  - No. 614 Squadron RAF Bristol Blenheim light bomber (laying smoke), RAF Inverness
- A squadron with Bristol Beaufighter
- No. 418 (City of Edmonton) Squadron RCAF Douglas Boston RAF Bradwell Bay
- No. 2 Group RAF (RAF Bomber Command)
  - No. 88 Squadron RAF Boston III, RAF Ford (tactical bombing)
  - No.107 Squadron RAF Boston III, RAF Ford (tactical bombing)
  - No. 226 Squadron RAF Boston III, RAF Thruxton (laying smoke)
- USAAF Eighth Air Force
  - 97th Bombardment Group (B-17Es), Grafton Underwood
    - 340th Bombardment Squadron, RAF Polebrook
    - 341st Bombardment Squadron, RAF Polebrook
    - 342nd Bombardment Squadron, RAF Grafton Underwood
    - 414th Bombardment Squadron, RAF Grafton Underwood
  - 31st Fighter Group (Spitfires)
    - 307th Fighter Squadron, RAF Biggin Hill
    - 308th Fighter Squadron, RAF Kenley
    - 309th Fighter Squadron, RAF Westhampnett

German Forces

- 302nd Static Infantry Division (Generalleutnant Konrad Haase), part of LXXXI Army Corps, Army Group D, defending the coast at Dieppe.
  - 570th Infantry Regiment
  - 571st Infantry Regiment
  - 572nd Infantry Regiment
  - 302nd Artillery Regiment
  - 302nd Reconnaissance Battalion
  - 302nd Antitank Battalion
  - 302nd Engineer Battalion
- 216th Battery
- 813th Battery
- 2/770 Army Coastal Battery
- Heavy Flak Group

Reserves not participating in the battle:

- 676th Infantry Regiment of the 332nd Static Infantry Division
- 10th Panzer Division
- SS Infantry Brigade *Leibstandarte Adolf Hitler*

Luftwaffe

- Jagdgeschwader 2 (2nd Fighter Wing)
- Jagdgeschwader 26 (26th Fighter Wing)
- Kampfgeschwader 2 (2nd Bomber Wing)
- II./Kampfgeschwader 40 (II. Group/40th Bomber Wing)
- I.(F)/123 Reconnaissance

APPENDIX B

Men of No. 3 Commando Killed at Dieppe

The following men were those members of No. 3 Commando who were killed during the raid. Shown against their names are the regiments with which they served prior to becoming Commandos.

Sapper Rex Alsager Adderley, Royal Engineers. No known grave and is commemorated on the Brookwood 1939-1945 Memorial.

Private Andrew Alexander Anderson, 22, Kings Own Scottish Borderers. Buried at the Abbeville Communal Cemetery Extension, Somme.

Private Cyril Ernest Barrett, 22, Oxford and Bucks Light Infantry. No known grave and is commemorated on the Brookwood 1939-1945 Memorial.

Private Fred Stanley Broadbent, 24, Royal Army Medical Corps. Buried at the Dieppe Canadian War Cemetery, Hautot-sur-Mer.

Private John Broster, Cheshire Regiment. Buried at the Newhaven Cemetery, Sussex.

Private John Robert Bryan, 35, Duke of Cornwall's Light Infantry. Buried at the Dieppe Canadian War Cemetery, Hautot-sur-Mer.

Gunner George William Cooper, 27, Royal Artillery. Buried at the Dieppe Canadian War Cemetery, Hautot-sur-Mer.

Private Douglas Morton Fisher, 22, 2nd Battalion (The London Scottish) Gordon Highlanders. Buried at the Dieppe Canadian War Cemetery, Hautot-sur-Mer.

Corporal Thomas Cecil Gerrard, 30, Royal Army Service Corps. No known grave and is commemorated on the Brookwood 1939-1945 Memorial.

Private Ernest Frank Harding, Devonshire Regiment. Buried at the Dieppe Canadian War Cemetery, Hautot-sur-Mer.

Lance Corporal Richard Harding, 22, Royal Armoured Corps. Buried at the Dieppe Canadian War Cemetery, Hautot-sur-Mer.

Private Norman Harrison, 22, South Staffordshire Regiment. No known grave and is commemorated on the Brookwood 1939-1945 Memorial.

Private Leonard Thomas Jackman, 22, Duke of Wellington's (West Riding) Regiment. No known grave and is commemorated on the Brookwood 1939-1945 Memorial.

Private John Anthony Lacey, 22, Royal Army Service Corps. Buried at the Pihen-Les-Guines War Cemetery, Pas de Calais.

Private Edward Roy Leddington, Duke of Cornwall's Light Infantry. No known grave and is commemorated on the Brookwood 1939-1945 Memorial.

Lance Serjeant Joseph Wallace Mills, 41, Bedfordshire and Hertfordshire Regiment. Buried at the Dieppe Canadian War Cemetery, Hautot-sur-Mer.

Fusilier Ernest Pickersgill, 29, Royal Scots Fusiliers. Buried at the Cayeux-Sur-Mer Communal Cemetery, Somme.

Private Francis Mons Rhodes, 27, Bedfordshire and Hertfordshire Regiment. Buried at the Dieppe Canadian War Cemetery, Hautot-sur-Mer.

Fusilier Thomas Robert Sharp, 29, Royal Scots Fusiliers. No known grave and is commemorated on the Brookwood 1939-1945 Memorial.

Gunner William Wall, 29, Royal Artillery. Buried at the Dieppe Canadian War Cemetery, Hautot-sur-Mer.

APPENDIX C

Men of the South Saskatchewan Regiment Killed at Dieppe

The Commonwealth War Graves Commission records the following information concerning men of the South Saskatchewan Regiment R.C.I.C who died or were killed as a result of their involvement in the raid on Dieppe.

Private Andrew Angus Allen
Private William Bahnuick
Private John Henry Lucien Bachleu
Private K.J. Bartlam
Private George Henry Bassett
Private Melville Douglas Beatty
Private Walter Earl Beatty
Private John Bish
Private Steven Borys
Lance Corporal George Frankland Brennand (DoW)
Private Robert John Burns
Private Arne Byklum
Private William Lorne Cameron

Private James Duncan Campbell
Lance Corporal Samuel Campbell
Private Robert Lloyd Carswell
Private Adelord Cayen (DoW)
Private Leonard Chilton
Private Walter Daniel Chymko
Sergeant Cyril Barnes Clark
Private James Arbuckle Clarke
Corporal Frank Clowes
Private Richard Collins
Lance Corporal Harvey Alfred Coulter
Private Gordon A. Danforth
Private William Danchuk
Private Leonard Owen Davies
Private William Wade Davison
Private Alexander Fotheringham Dawson
Private Dagnall Thomas Dempsey
Private Arthur Emperingham
Private Lynn Berdette Evernden
Corporal Leonard John Ford
Private Jules Alphonse Gagnon
Private Anthony Emil Joseph Gallant
Private Ernest Arthur William Harman
Private Joseph Heinz
Private Walter Celeste Heinzman
Private William Jasin
Private Frank Jewell
Private John Edward Johnstone
Private George F M Kammerer
Lieutenant Leonard George Kempton
Private Richard Ivan Kerr
Private Lorne Joseph King

MEN OF THE SOUTH SASKATCHEWAN REGIMENT KILLED AT DIEPPE

Private William James Knight
Private Cecil Robert Last
Private Stewart Laurie
Private Joseph Le Blanc
Private John David Mack
Private Colin MacDonald
Private William John Madden
Private Ralph Margetts
Corporal Graham Robertson Mavor
Warrant Officer Class II James Michael McAvoy
Sergeant James Roy McIntyre
Private William James Morrison
Private Trueman Norton
Private John Robert Papic
Private Raymond Ernest Pickford
Private Charles Frederick Pickney
Private Edward Joseph Poitras
Private Earl John Poole
Private David Everett Pow (DoW)
Private George Charles Redwood (DoW)
Private Herbert Daniel Richmond
Private Alden Joseph Rochon
Private John Spencer Rushmer
Lance Sergeant George Salmond
Privvate Ernest Sauter
Private Charles Edward Sawden
Private Leonard Lee Smith
Lance Sergeant Samuel Narcisess Joseph Smith
Private Hamilton Russell Stewart
Private William George Stainger
Private Walter David Taylor
Private Norman William Thomson

Private Fred Arthur Tromberg
Private Donald D J Tyman
Private George Thomas Underdahl
Private Clifford Walker
Private Robert Adams Wallace
Lance Corporal John Williams
Lieutenant Robert Andrew Woolard
Private John Thomas Winn

The two members of the South Saskatchewan Regiment R.C.I.C. who are showing as having died on 22 August 1942 must be the same two men referred to in the War Diary entry for 23 August:

Private Adelord Cayen
Private David Everett Pow

The Commonwealth War Graves Commission shows that between 23 August and 31 December 1942, a further two members of the South Saskatchewan Regiment had died from wounds sustained at Dieppe:

Lance Corporal George Charles Redwood
Acting Lance Corporal George Franklin Brennand

APPENDIX D

Men of the Queen's Own Cameron Highlanders of Canada Killed at Dieppe

Private Frederick W. Adams
Private Allen Scott Affleck
Private George Bayne
Private Alphonse Gaudias Belanger
Private Daniel Norman Benoit
Private Hugh Boal
Private Richard Carswell
Private Hugh Alfred Carver
Warrant Officer Class II Bert Connolly
Lance Corporal John Stewart Coulter
Private Harry Douglas
Private Robert Alan Drascovitch
Private James Anthony Duggan
Private Walter Dunkin
Private Robert Gordon Ferguson
Private Roger George Findlay

Sergeant Robert Fleming
Private Harold John Glenn
Lieuteant William Bryans Goodall
Lieutenant Colonel Alfred Capel Gostling
Private Carman Boyd Graham
Private John Graham
Sergeant Lewis Robley Graham
Private William James Greenaway
Private Charles Gilchrist Gunn
Private Vincent Giddard Hadfield
Private Allan C Hancock
Corporal Eldon Thornton P Hatch
Private Lester Heathman
Corporal Francis Rivers Gilbert Hicks
Private Jack James Hunter
Sergeant Leslie Ernest Hurst
Private Donald Joseph Galbraith Kirk
Private Andrew Joseph Laing
Private Richard Laird Leask
Sergeant William Benjamin Linklater
Private George Ernest Little
Private John Henry Finnis Madden
Private Lionel C. Marten
Private Henry Harold McFetridge
Corporal George W. McGhee
Lieutenant Alexander John McKellar
Private Edward Ewart McMahon
Lieutenant William McManus
Private Howard Gordon Miller
Private Martin Moore
Private William Edward O'Brien
Private Robert French Palmer

Sergeant Leslie Harold Pratt
Corporal Ralph Bertram Preece
Sergeant William Love Rankine
Private Herbert Ernie Rowe
Private Bernard Schacht
Private Eric William Sherritt
Private Stephen Skromeda
Private William A. St. Croix
Private Robert Edwin Stewart
Private Sidney Frederick Sutton
Private John Burton Tully
Lance Corporal Alfred John Vinie
Private Bennet Vincent Warne
Private George Charles Harvey West
Private Duncan Cameron Wilson
Lieutenant Richard Ambrose Wise
Captain Norman Andrew Thomson Young

The following men subsequently died of wounds sustained during the raid on Dieppe:

Private Ernest Albert Shakeshaft. Died 20 August 1942.
Corporal Thomas Duncan Gordon McLeod. Died 21 August 1942.
Private Victor Horton. Died 21 August 1942.
Private William Joseph Mowat. Died 24 August 1942.
Warrant Officer Class II Kenneth Ivan McAmmond. Died 29 August 1942.
Private Ernest William Horner. Died 13 September 1942.
Private Robert Arnold King. Died 26 September 1942.
Private Edmond Christofferson. Died 5 October 1942.
Private John Alexander Forsythe. Died 5 October 1942.
Private James Earl Phillips. Died 30 October 1942.

APPENDIX E

Men of the Black Watch (Royal Highland Regiment of Canada) Killed at Dieppe

Five members of the Black Watch are recorded as having been killed in action or died of their wounds as a result of their involvement in the raid on Dieppe.

Private Oswald Raymond Boyd (DoW)
Lieutenant John David Colson
Private Walter James Graham (DoW)
Private Gordon Thomas Harwood (DoW)
Captain John Alexander Kenny

Decorations Awarded Following the Dieppe Raid

Victoria Cross

Captain Patrick Porteous, Royal Regiment of Artillery, attached to No. 4 Commando

Reverend John Weir Foote, Padre to the Royal Hamilton Light Infantry

Lieutenant Colonel Charles Merritt, South Saskatchewan Regiment

Conspicuous Gallantry Medal

Ordinary Seaman Thomas Albert Lee of the Royal Navy deserves a special mention for his individual act of bravery at Dieppe, which undoubtedly saved the lives of a large number of Canadian soldiers. The landing craft Lee was on board, on which he was a gunner, made it to the beach at Dieppe. Here is the citation for his award which appeared in the *London Gazette* of 2 October 1942.

While the craft in which Ordinary Seaman Lee was serving was beached for some fifteen minutes landing tanks, under concentrated fire, her guns were kept in action against an enemy gun position and houses on the beach, until all the guns crews had been killed or wounded. Although gravely wounded himself, his cheerful courage and devotion to duty were an example to the rest. He carried on until the guns were silenced and then crawled away to report to his skipper.

Distinguished Service Order

Lieutenant Colonel Robert Douglas King, The Princess Louise Fusiliers (Motor)

Lieutenant Colonel Dollard Menard, Les Fusiliers Mont-Royal

Acting Lieutenant Colonel Lord Lovat, No. 4 Commando

Major General John Hamilton Roberts, M.C., Commanding Officer, 2nd Canadian Infantry Division (in his command ship in the waters off Dieppe)

Brigadier Sherwood Lett, M.C. South Saskatchewan Regiment

Brigadier Clarence Churchill Mann, Deputy Military Force Commander

Major John Begg, 14th Canadian Army Tank Regiment (The Calgary Regiment (Tank)) Canadian Armoured Corps

Major Douglas Gordon Cunningham, The Queen's Own Cameron Highlanders of Canada

Major Arthur Hayward Fraser, Princess Patricia's Canadian Light Infantry

Major Andrew Thompson Law, The Queen's Own Cameron Highlanders of Canada

Major James Earl McRae, The South Saskatchewan Regiment
Captain Marie-Edmond Paul Garneau, Royal Canadian Regiment
Captain William Denis Whitaker, The Royal Hamilton Light Infantry (Wentworth Regiment)

Military Cross

Captain Laurence Guy Alexander, Royal Canadian Army Medical Corps
Captain John Charles Holtby Anderson, The Regiment of Canada
Captain James Porter Browne, Canadian Chaplain Service
Captain Harvey Barnet Carswell, The Royal Canadian Artillery
Captain Francis Wilfred Hayter, Royal Canadian Army Medical Corps
Captain Hugh John Kennedy, The Essex Scottish
Captain Robert Hector Lajoie, Les Fusiliers Mont-Royal
Captain Donald Fraser MacRae, The Stormonf Dundas and Glengarry Highlanders
Captain Ronald John Wilkinson, The South Saskatchewan Regiment
Lieutenant Pierre Benoit, Les Fusiliers Mont-Royal
Lieutenant John Gibbons Counsell, The Royal Hamilton Light Infantry (Wentworth Regiment)
Lieutenant John Blake Gartshore, The Royal Hamilton Light Infantry (Wentworth Regiment)
Lieutenant Arthur Charles Kavanaugh, The Queen's Own Cameron Highlanders of Canada
Lieutenant Paul Pierre Loranger, Les Fusiliers Mont-Royal
Lieutenant Joseph Edward Ernest McManus, The Queen's Own Cameron Highlanders of Canada

Distinguished Conduct Medal

Private William Alvin Haggard, South Saskatchewan Regiment (also received a field promotion to the rank of lieutenant)

Regimental Sergeant Major Rosario Levesque, Les Fusiliers Mont-Royal

Company Sergeant Major George Gouk, The Queen's Own Cameron Highlanders of Canada

Company Sergeant Major Jack Stewart, The Royal Hamilton Light Infantry (Wentworth Regiment)

Sergeant Ernest Elmer Gordon, The Queen's Own Cameron Highlanders of Canada

Lance Sergeant George Alfred Hickson, The Corps of Royal Canadian Engineers

Corporal Adam Brygider, The Queen's Own Cameron Highlanders of Canada

Lance Corporal Guy Bernard Berthelot, The South Saskatchewan Regiment

Lance Corporal Leslie George Ellis, The Royal Regiment of Canada

Lance Corporal Milton Douglas Sinasac, The Corps of Royal Canadian Engineers

Private Thomas William Graham, The Royal Hamilton Light Infantry (Wentworth Regiment)

Private James Maier, The Essex Scottish

Military Medal

Company Sergeant Major William Joseph Dean, The Royal Hamilton Light Infantry (Wentworth Regiment)

Sergeant Pierre Dubuc, Les Fusiliers Mont-Royal

Sergeant Wilfred Gagne, Les Fusiliers Mont-Royal

Sergeant David Lloyd Hart, The Royal Canadian Corps of Signals
Sergeant Waldron Edward Hussey, The Essex Scottish
Sergeant John Edgar Legate, The Royal Regiment of Canada
Sergeant John William Marsh, The Black Watch (Royal Highland Regiment) of Canada
Sergeant Albert Edward Mundy, The South Saskatchewan Regiment
Sergeant Ernest Thirgood, The Royal Regiment of Canada
Acting Sergeant Earl Kitchener Skippon, The Corps of Royal Canadian Engineers
Lance Sergeant Frank Leslie Dixon, The Essex Scottish
Corporal Robert Berube, Les Fusiliers Mont-Royal
Corporal Robert Carle, The Essex Scottish
Corporal Joseph Arthur Gregory, The South Saskatchewan Regiment
Corporal Walter Harry Gibson, Les Fusiliers Mont-Royal
Corporal Alexander Keller, The Queen's Own Cameron Highlanders of Canada
Corporal Frank Koons (US Army Ranger) (The first American soldier to be awarded a British medal for bravery during the course of the Second World War)
Corporal Frederick Harold Ruggles, The Royal Regiment of Canada
Lance Corporal Calvin Wilbert John Helmer, 14 Canadian Tank Regiment (The Calgary Regiment (Tank), Canadian Armoured Corps
Lance Corporal George Thomas Nugent, The Queen's Own Cameron Highlanders of Scotland
Lance Corporal John Fisher, The Corps of Royal Canadian Engineers

Lance Corporal Stanley Earl Gilbert, The Royal Canadian Corps of Signals
Lance Corporal George Alfred McDermott, The Royal Hamilton Light Infantry (Wentworth Regiment)
Gunner Henry John Rowe, The Royal Canadian Artillery
Private Thomas Patrick Bibby, The Royal Canadian Army Medical Corps
Private Alexander Stuart Chisholm, The Toronto Scottish Regiment (M.G.)
Private Walter Duggan, The Royal Regiment of Canada
Private Leo David De Laurier, The Essex Scottish
Private Cecil Harold Dyke, The Royal Hamilton Light Infantry (Wentworth Regiment)
Private Oliver Odeen Fenner, The South Saskatchewan Regiment
Private Leo Filiault, Les Fusiliers Mont-Royal
Private Jack James Hunter, The Queen's Own Cameron Highlanders of Scotland
Private Alexander Huppe, The Queen's Own Cameron Highlanders of Scotland
Private Fernand Labrecque, Les Fusiliers Mont-Royal
Private George Edmond Marchant, The Essex Scottish
Private William Carnegie McKellar, The South Saskatchewan Regiment
Private William George McLennan, The Royal Regiment of Canada
Private Thomas McQuade, The Royal Hamilton Light Infantry (Wentworth Regiment)
Private Leonard Allan Middleton, The Toronto Scottish Regiment (M.G.)
Private John Henry Mizon, The Essex Scottish
Private Robert Arthur Montague, The Essex Scottish

Private James Murphy, The Royal Regiment of Canada
Private Leslie Robert Thrussell, The South Saskatchewan Regiment
Private William Vergette, The Royal Hamilton Light Infantry (Wentworth Regiment)
Signalman William John Ray, The Royal Canadian Corps of Signals

Distinguished Flying Cross

Flying Officer George Allan Casey, Royal Canadian Air Force

Distinguished Flying Medal

Sergeant Clarence Garfield Scott, Royal Canadian Air Force

Bar to Distinguished Flying Cross

Acting Squadron Leader Leslie Sidney Ford, D.F.C., Royal Canadian Air Force

Mentioned in Recognition of Gallant and Distinguished Services

This recognition was bestowed upon a total of ninety-three men from fifteen separate Canadian Regiments for their actions at Dieppe. The full details of which can be found in the *London Gazette* of 2 October 1942, supplement number 35729, pages 4330-1.

Certificate

All those who participated in the raid were awarded a certificate of thanks by the Government of France.

Volunteer Service Medal

In 1980, the Canadian Government, belated awarded all surviving veterans of the raid on Dieppe, a volunteer service medal.

APPENDIX G

French Civilians Killed in the Dieppe Raid

The following is a list of names of French civilians who were killed during the course of the Raid on Dieppe.

Basly, Alexandre, 29
Bezirad, Marie, 46
Bidard, Jean, 22
Bouvier, Cecile, 8
Brunet, Lucienne, 25
Brunet, Roger, 16
Bureau, Angele, 59
Burette, Madeleine, 52
Castelin, Aristide, 70
Claire, Louis, 89
Clermont, Louise, 19
Conseil, Andre, 37
Cousin, Henri, 55
Debonne, Eugenie, 55
De Hayes, Auguste, 56
De Hayes, Edouard, 50

Duval, Yvonne, 29
Elluin, Albertine, 39
Freville, Claude, 3
Gaillardon, Charles, 17
Gallene, Rene, 22
Gautier, Clemence, 51
Giffard, Gabrielle, 44
Godalier, Senateur, 52
Gode, Fernard, 31
Gorce, Jean, 18
Goye, Suazanne, 55
Grout, Arthur, 50
Grout, Joseph (no age given)
Gueno, Pierre, 7
Huray, Marcel, 15
Huray, Raymond, 15
Hurel, Emile, 49
Lemarchand, Madeleine, 52
Lequien, Louis, 37
Leroux, Fernand, 37
Levasseur, Paul, 54
Lorphelan, Marcel, 22
Magnier, Marguerite, 20
Magnier, Andre, 16
Magnier, Charles, 50
Menival, Bernard, 13
Meunier, Clemence (no age given)
Pegard, Albertine, 17
Samson, Albert, 38
Sautrel, Jean, 16
Verel, Alban, 46
Ying Pong, Sui, 51

Sources

www.thecanadianencyclopedia.ca
www.thegazette.co.uk
www.warhistoryonline.com
www.dieppe-operationjubilee-19aout1942.fr
www.cwgc.com
www.britishnewspaperarchive.co.uk
www.canada.ca
www.commandoveterans.org
www.nationalww2museum.org
www.legionmagazine.com
www.cbc.ca
www.combinedops.com
www.tributes.com
www.iirangers.org
www.arsof-history.org
Library and Archives Canada
www.saskatchewanmilitarymuseum.ca
www.defence.gov.au
www.historynet.com
www.repository.cam.ac.uk
www.vconline.org.uk

About the Author

Stephen is a happily retired police officer having served with Essex Police as a constable for thirty years between 1983 and 2013. He is married to Tanya, who is also his best friend.

Both his sons, Luke and Ross, were members of the armed forces, collectively serving five tours of Afghanistan between 2008 and 2013. Both were injured on their first tour. This led to Stephen's first book *Two Sons in a Warzone – Afghanistan: The True Story of a Fathers Conflict*, which was published in October 2010.

Both of Stephen's grandfathers served in and survived the First World War, one with the Royal Irish Rifles, the other in the Mercantile Navy, whilst his father was a member of the Royal Army Ordinance Corp during and after the Second World War.

Stephen corroborated with one of his writing partners, Ken Porter, on a previous book published in August 2012, *German POW Camp 266 – Langdon Hills*. They have also collaborated on four books in the 'Towns & Cities in the Great War' series by Pen and Sword.

Stephen has co-written three crime thrillers which were published between 2010 and 2012, and centre round a fictional detective named Terry Danvers.

When he is not writing, Stephen and Tanya enjoy the simplicity of going out for a morning coffee, lunch time meals or walking their four German shepherd dogs early each morning, whilst most sensible people are still fast asleep in their beds.

Other works for Pen & Sword include:

The Surrender of Singapore: Three Years of Hell 1942-45 (2017)
Against All Odds: Walter Tull, the Black Lieutenant (2018)
Animals in the Great War (2018) (co-written with Tanya Wynn)
A History of the Royal Hospital Chelsea – 1682-2017: The Warriors' Repose (2019) (co-written with Tanya Wynn)
Disaster before D-Day: Unravelling the Tragedy of Slapton Sands (2019)
Countering Hitler's Spies - British Military Intelligence 1940-1945 (2020)
Mystery of Missing Flight F-BELV (2020)
Holocaust: The Nazis' Wartime Jewish Atrocities (2020)
Churchill's Flawed Decisions: Errors in Office of the Greatest Britain (2020)
The Lancastria Tragedy: Sinking and Cover-up 1940 (2020)
The Shetland 'Bus': Transporting Secret Agents Across the North Sea (2021)
Dunkirk and the Aftermath (2021)
St Nazaire Raid, 1942 (2022)
The Blackout Ripper: A Serial Killer in London, 1942 (2022)
HMS Turbulent (2023)

Index

Alvoet, Private Jerome Gerard, 128
Army Tank Regiment, 17, 30, 38, 85, 141

Beach, Blue, 31, 36-7, 91, 177-8
Beach Comber, 201-204
Beach, Green, 31, 40, 45, 91
Beach, Orange, 31, 44
Beach, Red, 31, 38, 91, 141, 177
Beach, White, 31, 38, 91, 141
Beach, Yellow, 31-4, 153, 154
Black Watch (Royal Highland Regiment) of Canada, 36-7, 91
Brocklesby, HMS, 33, 57
Burette, Madeleine, 69

Catanach, James, 84
Chain Home, 32
Christensen, Flight Lieutenant Arnold George, 82-4

Churchill, Winston, 1-3, 7, 12-13, 15-16, 108, 125-7, 133, 165-6, 194-5, 200, 207-208
Cloutier, Private Gerard, 103-104
Combined Operations, 112-15, 145, 149-50, 152, 159, 163, 169, 194, 198
Cordite, Operation, 11
Crerar, DSO, Lieutenant Colonel H. D. G., 198-9

Darby, Captain Willian Orlando, 62-4
Decorations Awarded for Dieppe, 235-41
Defence of the Realm Act, 202
Durnford-Slater, Lieutenant Colonel John, 141, 152-3, 217

Eden, Sir Anthony, 24
Enigma, 134

Espelid, Halldor, 84
Essex Scottish Regiment, 17, 30, 38, 85, 128, 141, 176-8

First Moscow Conference, 12
Forces Deployed at Dieppe, 216-23
Foote, Honorary Captain John Weir, 98-100
Ford I, II and III, Exercise(s), 171
Fraser, Lieutenant Colonel Simon (Lord Lovat), 44, 73, 77, 95-6, 141, 186, 217
French Civilians killed at Dieppe, 242-3
Fuglesang, Nils Jørgen, 84

Gode, Fernand, 69
Goebbels, Joseph, 76, 109, 141
Grout, Joseph, 69

Haase, Generalleutnant Konrad, 72
Hawkins, Sergeant Roy, 48, 58
Henry III, Hugh G., 192, 193, 197, 199, 200
Hess, Rudolf, 76
Hindenburg, Paul von, 76

Houghton, Major General Robert Dyer "Titch", 137
Hughes-Hallett, Captain John, 1, 6, 7, 171, 217

Jacobs, Company Sergeant Major William, 103
Jones, Professor Reginald V, 60
Josephine Charlotte, HMS, 20
Jubilee, Operation, ix, 1, 10, 11, 14, 17, 21-2, 27, 38, 48, 67, 145-7, 151, 153, 167, 171, 173, 191

Keyes, Admiral of the Fleet Roger, 3
Kieffer, Captain Philippe, 139

Labatt, Lieutenant Colonel R. R., 177
Lawrence, Major Jock, 149, 198
Laycock, Major General Sir Robert, 3
Lee, Lieutenant L D, 175, 176
Lee, CGM, Ordinary Seaman Thomas Albert, 101, 180, 184

Leigh-Mallory, Air Chief Marshall Sir Trafford, 2, 9, 22, 23, 28, 171
Les Fusiliers Mont-Royal, 17, 30, 85, 103, 139-41, 143, 156-7, 176, 179, 209

Mann, Lieutenant Colonel Churchill C., 162-3, 165
McDonald, Lieutenant, 95
McNaughton, General Andrew George Latta, 149, 170-1, 196
Ménard, Lieutenant Colonel, Dollard, 142, 156
Merritt, VC, Lieutenant Colonel Charles, 41-2, 48, 52, 59, 90-4, 100
Meunier, Clemence, 70
Mills-Roberts, Major Derek, 73, 95
Montgomery, Lieutenant General Bernard, 2, 6, 20, 66, 153, 169, 192-3
Mountbatten, Admiral Louis, 1, 4, 7, 22-3, 30, 66, 112, 145, 149, 153, 169, 171-2, 193-200, 208

Nissenthall, RAF Flight Sergeant Jack, 45-2, 54-6, 58-61, 209

No. 3 Commando, 30, 32, 34, 66, 127, 140-1, 143, 224-6
No. 4 Commando, 30, 44, 77, 94-5, 127, 140-2
No. 10 Commando, 30, 127, 140, 172
No. 30 Commando, 30, 127, 135
No. 40 Commando, 30, 127, 135-8, 156

Osten, Captain Thomas Murray, 54

Pettiward, Captain, 95
Phillipps, Lieutenant Colonel J. P., 137-8, 210
Popsy, Exercise, 171
Porteous, VC, Major Patrick Anthony, 94-8
Pound, First Sea Lord, Sir Dudley, 30-1
Princess Astrid, HMS, 20-1

Queen's Own Cameron Highlanders of Canada, 17, 40, 43, 77, 91, 154, 171, 176, 178, 212, 231-3

Rivait, Alphonse, 87-9
Rivait, Lawrence, 87-9
Rivait, Leon, 87-9

Rivait, Raymond, 87-9
Roberts, Major General John Hamilton, 2, 7, 8, 9, 22, 86, 141, 149-50, 156, 171
Rogers, Lieutenant John Edward, 102
Rommel, General Erwin, 76
Royal Hamilton Light Infantry, 17, 30, 38, 85-6, 98, 100, 141, 176, 178
Royal Regiment of Canada, 17, 30, 36-7, 91, 103, 176-8
Rutter, Operation, 14, 17, 20-2, 28, 38, 153, 162, 166-7, 170, 192

Sinclair, Admiral Sir Hugh, 135
Slazak, ORP, 33
South Saskatchewan Regiment, 17, 40, 42-3, 45, 49, 52-3, 91, 154, 176, 227-30
Southam, Brigadier William Wallace, 79, 130-1, 174-8
Stacey, Major, Charles Perry, 144, 148, 150-1, 163, 170, 172, 176-8, 196, 198-9
Stockdale, Troop Sergeant Major, 95

Tait, Air Commodore Victor Hubert, 60
Tangmere, RAF, 172
The Black Watch (Royal Highland Regiment), 36-7, 91, 216, 234
Truscott, Lieutenant Colonel Lucian K., 63

US Army Rangers, 1st Battalion, 30, 44, 62-5, 111-12, 123, 127, 217

Vaughan, MBE, Colonel Charles, 62
von Rundstedt, Field Marshal Gerd, 107
Vourch, Lieutenant Guy, 179

Wehl, Mr David, 129
Willis, Captain R. L., 154
Wood, Lieutenant, J. E. R., 179

Young, Captain Peter, 154
Yukon I, Exercise, 19-20, 153, 169
Yukon II, Exercise, 152, 169